2008

The Meanest Man in Patrick County

and Other Unlikely Brethren Heroes

Frank Ramirez

Brethren Press

The Meanest Man in Patrick County
and Other Unlikely Brethren Heroes
Frank Ramirez

Copyright 2004 Frank Ramirez.
Published by Brethren Press®, 1451 Dundee Avenue, Elgin, IL
60120. Brethren Press is a program of the Church of the
Brethren General Board.

Cover design by Gwen M. Stamm

Library of Congress Control Number: 2004104442
ISBN: 0-87178-059-3

08 07 06   5 4 3 2

Printed in the United States of America

This book is one of several Brethren Press publications
displaying the mark of the 300th anniversary of the Brethren
(1708-2008). It represents the theme "Surrendered to God,
Transformed by Christ, Empowered by the Spirit."

To my son Jacob Ramirez,
who listened to a lot of my stories
and told more than his share as well.

Out to the Sea

Out to the sea in a boat we came
Though the waters were wild and deep
The Lord we served is still the same
And every dream will keep.
    Buried within the hold the smoke
    Of cooking fires would darkly fume
    Until we feared that all would choke.
    Yet always will our prayers resume.
Near death the old and very young
Are hovering, while angels' wings
Like rushing clouds are heard among
The notes that rise as one more sings.
    The waves will toss the ship about
    Until with sickness, dread, and fear
    And rank despair some came to doubt.
    But always God is standing near.
Yet in the end the sight of land,
And with it joy and hope fulfilled,
Restored our faith that all was planned.
Belief in God was reinstilled.   *F.R.*

Contents

1
Wading into Danger
The First Brethren Baptism

Schwarzenau, Germany, 1708

"What will they will do to us if they catch us?" Joanna Boni asked.

It was early morning. The air was so still that even sounds from far away sounded very close. She could hear the lowing of a cow, wanting to be milked. A dog was barking. Perhaps it was hungry, or perhaps it could hear the women walking along the country road. It was too early for most people in the town to be out and about, but for farmers, of course, work had already started.

Joanna Boni looked over her shoulder again at her companions. There were two other women, Joanna Kipping and Anna Margaretha Mack, walking with her to the Eder River, which flowed near the town of Schwarzenau in Germany.

They were going to the river to be baptized, which was against the law in their country.

"They used to drown people for getting baptized," Anna said. "That's what it says in the big book that Brother Alexander keeps in our home right next to the Bible."

Brother Alexander was Alexander Mack, who helped lead illegal Bible studies in his home. These people who studied the Bible together called each other brother and sister, and together they called themselves Brethren.

There had been rain the night before and it was a little muddy. The three women walked carefully, looking for stepping stones or dry spots of ground. So it was a moment before Joanna Kipping said, "Was that book the *Martyrs' Mirror*?"

"Yes," Anna said. "It's the book that tells how God's people have suffered for staying faithful to the Bible."

"That's what makes us God's people," Joanna Kipping added. "Are we almost there?"

The dog barked again, and Joanna Boni jumped and nearly lost her balance. They all laughed.

"I guess we are all a little nervous," she said. "But we've all suffered before."

"That's right," Anna said. "I remember that before you married Andrew he was put in prison for a time."

"And later they put him in the pillory." Joanna Boni said. "They locked his head and hands in the stocks right in front of everyone so they could mock him. That was after his first wife and my first husband had died. We were pledged to be married then."

"And you," Anna said to Joanna Kipping, "they tried to take your children away from you because you would not baptize them as infants. That was very brave of you."

"It was a very bad time. John had to flee the town, and for awhile I was alone with the children. Everyone in our village looked down on us. We lost our home—we lost everything. They tried to make us ashamed of the gospel. They said we must not care about our children and that we were bad people. But, praise God, we were able to come together again, even though it is so far from our home. And you lost your home, too, didn't you, Anna?"

"Yes. That was a terrible night when the authorities came to our house because we were holding a Bible study. They said we had no right to study the Bible by ourselves. We had to pack everything up and flee with what we could carry. We lost a lot that night, but then we have all lost so much."

The women could hear the river clearly now, the water lapping over the stones. Soon they would reach this place, as they had resolved together just a few nights ago. There were eight of them, the three women and the five men who were following behind them.

Anna wished there were more of them. Only a few days before, their group had decided that the Bible called for baptism in the water, baptism by people old enough to make up their own minds to follow Jesus. But some of their group had left them because they disagreed. Some left because they were afraid. And others said they did not want to break the law, even if it was a bad law.

In those days all of Europe had been torn by religious wars, with Christians fighting other Christians who did not believe as they did. Following the wars a treaty was signed saying that people had to belong to the same church as their local ruler, which would be either Catholic, Lutheran, or Reformed.

These churches were often more concerned with their own power and wealth than with the suffering of the people, many of whom had lost everything in the wars or had been driven from one land to another. These churches had many practices and beliefs that could not be found in the Bible.

As a result, many people were reading the Bible on their own and wanted the freedom to follow God in their own way, but the law demanded they go to a church whose beliefs might not be like their own. Some of these people were driven from city to city, even though they were honest people who worked hard and shared with others.

These eight people about to be baptized believed that Jesus wanted a visible church like the early church Jesus started. Therefore, they would do only those things called for in the Bible. And the first thing that church would require was baptism by people who made their own choice to be baptized. They had all been baptized as babies, but that baptism had been done for them, when they could not choose. The eight of them together, reading their Bibles and arguing and sharing, wanted to be baptized through their own choice, even if it meant they would have to break the country's law in order to follow God's law.

Knowing that in the past Christians had killed other Christians by drowning them or burning them or by some other horrible way, the three women were wondering what might happen next to them.

"What if one of those who left us has told the authorities?" Joanna Boni wondered out loud. "What if there are spies looking at us?"

"Even if that were so," Anna asked, "would that change what we are about to do?"

"No," she answered. "I read the Bible the same as you. Jesus was baptized by John the Baptist when he was grown up. And in the Acts of the Apostles, Cornelius the Centurion and Lydia, the businesswoman who owned the purple dye, and all the others were baptized when they were old enough to make up their own minds. Nowhere do we find one word about babies being baptized."

"That's right," Joanna Kipping said. "Babies already belong to God. God loves them. We offer them to God, but they do not need to be baptized until they are old enough to know right from wrong. And that terrible minister, telling us that they were evil and sinful and lost, that if they died they would go to hell unless they were baptized. I am still angry when I think of him."

"The Lord Jesus told us to love our enemies and do good to those who persecute us," Anna said. "We must try to love those who hurt us."

"I know, I know," admitted Joanna.

Now they stood by the water's edge. "There's no turning back. Not for us," Joanna Boni said. "Let's get ready."

The three women looked for a small grove of trees nearby. "This will do," Anna said as she unfolded some large bed sheets, which the women hung from the trees. They stepped behind the sheets and quickly changed into robes. They then stacked some towels nearby.

"Listen," Anna said. "I can hear the men following. They make such a racket."

"Yes," Joanna Boni laughed. "If the spies weren't sure how to find us, they would know now."

"Unless those are the spies you hear," Joanna Kipping warned. For a moment the three women were silent.

"What if we are arrested before we are even baptized?" Joanna Boni asked. "Please God, spare us until we are obedient to your word," she prayed.

"There are many things that will never come to pass," Anna said. "Each of us has seen our lives changed by fortune or misfortune. I know my Alexander wanted to go to the university, but when his brother died he became the town miller instead. And you have all lost an honest living or a home. God knows we have sacrificed so much, and God will understand if we are arrested now."

"God grant we are baptized before we are arrested," Joanna Kipping prayed.

"Hello!" called out a man's voice, and Anna smiled.

"That's my Alexander," she said. "I know his voice anywhere. We are here! We are ready!"

The women stepped out in their robes, as the five men walked up. There was Alexander Mack, and John Kipping, and Andrew Boni, along with two other men, Georg Grebe and Lukas Vetter. They were all men who had honorable trades.

The men took their turn behind the sheets, singing a hymn together as they changed into their robes.

"Less singing, more haste," Anna said. "You men are very slow." She heard the men laugh. When they emerged the eight took a moment to look at each other.

"A fine party we are," Anna said. "All in our robes, all ready to get wet. It is at least as fine a summer morning as we could ask for."

"I want to remind us all why we are here," her husband, Alexander, said. He held in his hands a large Bible, and with a quick, practiced movement, he found the page he sought.

"At the end of Matthew's Gospel, we read that Jesus told his disciples that they should go forth into all the world and baptize others in the name of the Father, and of the Son, and of the Holy Spirit. This is a scripture we have studied together, and we have decided together, the eight of us, that if we are to be baptized, it must be by immersion, by being completely covered with water three times, in the name of the Father, and of the Son, and of the Holy Spirit. Are you still agreed on that?"

The other seven nodded.

"I'm a little nervous," Joanna Boni added. "May we not be baptized before we are all taken away by the authorities? This is a lot of talking."

"I'm as nervous as the rest of you," Alexander said, "but we must be certain that we are in agreement on this. And as for any arrest, we should not be surprised, for we also read in the Gospel that Jesus told his disciples they would be persecuted in his name, but that there would be no one who has lost mother, father, brother, sister, house, and lands for his sake and for the sake of the gospel who will not receive a hundredfold what they lost."

"Then we shall all be very wealthy in God's kingdom" Joanna Kipping laughed, as did the others. "But who will perform the baptisms? Who will be our John the Baptist?"

"We have decided that Alexander shall be called as our first minister," Georg said. "And he shall baptize the rest of us."

"I know that," Joanna Kipping. "But who will baptize him?"

"As to that," Alexander said, "we prayed about that on our way here and have decided that the four men will draw lots and that one of them will baptize me before I baptize all of you. And we have decided also that none of us shall ever reveal who it was who performed that first baptism."

"Why not?" asked Anna.

"So that we will not be named after someone who is considered our leader," Alexander replied. "That is the folly the Apostle Paul warned us about in his first letter to the Corinthians. We are not to take our name from other people, or to take pride in who baptized us. We are not starting a new church, after all, but calling all people back to the original church of Jesus Christ. We are brothers and sisters, we are Brethren who love Jesus, and nothing more. And we come here willingly. We have counted the cost of what it means to follow Jesus. All of us have lost something. And all of us want to gain new life in Jesus Christ.

"In our Bible study together, we have decided that to be the church of Jesus we must practice the feetwashing and the meal known as the love feast with our communion. We will anoint each other with oil for healing. We will lay hands on each other in prayer. And we will correct each other when it is needed, for none of us is perfect, none of us is greater than the other. All of us are called to be ministers of the gospel in our baptism. And the first step to all of this is this baptism."

The men then stepped to the side and looked for small stones, each picking one that was different and easily recognizable. One of the men put the stones in a hat. He shook the hat until a single stone fell out.

The man whose stone fell out paused for a moment. All were silent.

Then Anna began to sing, and the others sang with her. They liked to sing together. Sometimes it was a hymn they had learned from others. Other times it was one they had written themselves. They were writing many new hymns to express their excitement, their new life in Jesus.

Picking up a long branch, Alexander Mack stepped out into the river. The water splashed around his ankles, then his knees, and finally his waist. He measured the water with the stick until he found a deep and level spot.

"Come in," he called to the one whose stone had fallen out of the hat. Alexander knelt down, resting on his heels. Suddenly the sun rose above the treetops and shone brightly around the two in the water. In the minutes before dawn, Anna had grown used to the muted colors of the world that waited for day, but now every color was brighter. Every tree, every leaf on those trees, became awash with color and light. Their gray tones gave way to browns and greens. There were little caps of white on the water that spilled around the two in the river. Anna wondered if this is what it had looked like when Jesus stepped into the water and knelt next to John the Baptist. For a moment all time was frozen.

"If you are willing to renounce the world and the devil and your own flesh, then answer with yes," said the man standing in the water.

"Yes," Alexander said.

Pushing Alexander's head under the water three times, the man said, "I baptize you in the name of God the Father, the Son, and the Holy Spirit."

Anna was surprised it all happened so quickly. Here was the beginning of a new world, of a people dedicated to God. Her husband was spluttering and shaking his head, rubbing his eyes, but smiling, even laughing.

"I think it will be better if we remember to keep our mouth and nose closed!" he said to those on shore.

Quickly he baptized the man who had baptized him. The other three men followed in short order. The three women took a moment, wondering which of them should follow.

"I'll go first," Anna said. She took a step into the water.

As a little girl she had loved to play in rivers and streams, but it had been many years since those days and she had rarely gone into the water. Anna was surprised at how cold it was. She almost stepped back without thinking.

"I am not afraid of the authorities," she thought to herself. "I'm not afraid of being arrested. I will not be worried by the cold."

As she knelt in the water, she held on to her husband's hand, afraid she might be swept away. The river flowed around her and she started to shiver. But she felt secure now.

"If you are willing to renounce the world and the devil and your own flesh," Alexander said, "then answer…"

"Yes," she replied, before he could finish, and then thought to herself she had better close her mouth. Whoosh! She was under the water, in the darkness of the water like

Jonah. Then she was up again, and the light was bright around her.

"...Son, and of the..." she heard Alexander say, and then she was under the water again, and up, and under again. The water felt pure, churning all around her, clean and sharp and alive. Jesus had offered the woman Living Water, Anna thought to herself, and now it occurred to her that the water might be alive, rushing, changing their lives, carving out new channels in history, and always remaining true to itself.

All in a moment she thought these things, and then she was standing up and smiling. She could hear the others singing more of the same hymn she'd begun.

Anna walked back to the shore but stayed standing, her feet still in the water, reluctant to leave the river behind now that it had become a place for new life. One by one the other two women followed. No matter what happens now, she thought to herself, no matter how much we suffer, no matter to what strange land we must flee, nothing can take away our baptism or our love of Jesus.

At last, when they had all changed back into their clothes, they walked away from the river. Their hair was still wet, but the summer's sun would take care of that. Already the day was no longer young. There would be much to do. They were planning a meal taken together in celebration, and after that more prayer and singing.

"Nothing will be the same," Joanna Boni said. "Nothing can ever be the same."

"I guess the spies forgot to come," Anna said.

"Or maybe they've gone to the wrong place," Joanna Kipping laughed.

"I'm sure trials lie ahead, but I am so glad to have been baptized this morning. It feels like a new life," Anna said. "No matter what happens to us, God will be with us on the journey. God will always be with us."

The brothers and sisters who called themselves Brethren indeed continued to struggle. They moved from place to place, sharing what money they had until little or none was left. Some were imprisoned. Others were tortured. Some were forced into hard labor. But always they stayed faithful. And their group grew. Many more were baptized. Almost all of them eventually sailed to Pennsylvania for the religious freedom to practice the faith they found in the Bible. But that is another story.

2
Voyage to Freedom
A Letter to a Friend

Germantown, Pennsylvania
October 1, 1733

Dear Willy:
Remember the fruit seller in the market-
place in Krefeld and how you and I
would often stand together looking at
the apples and pears and strawberries?
Remember the oranges and how we
wondered what they would taste like
and wished it were a holiday so our parents would buy one for us?

And what about when we got one of those apples?
Remember how crisp it could be and how we used to eat all
of it, every little bit, until there was just the stem and a tiny
bit of core with the seeds in the middle?

Well, I want to tell you about America—about the pears
and cherries and apples. I want to tell you about the sweet-
est apple I have ever tasted and that these apples don't cost

13

anything. But these apples are very hard to get, because you have to go on a very dangerous voyage, and not everyone survives the trip to get these apples. But if you get here to America, with God's grace, then you can have one of these apples too.

I don't know if we'll ever see each other again in this world, or if we must wait until God sees fit to bring us together in heaven, but I want to tell you about our trip to America! Yes, we are in Pennsylvania, Willy, and we are living in this place that was just a dream for many people. But there are many Brethren here in the city they have named for us—Germantown.

Unlike the law in Europe that said we must attend one of the three official churches, whichever one our local ruler attended, here in Pennsylvania we are free to worship wherever we want, after the manner of what we have learned in the Bible.

I hope you and your sister and your father are doing well, and your father's new wife. I was sorry to hear your mother died of the flu. I know you are all working hard, like we did, digging up the peat to sell for fuel. The Mennonites were very kind to us, helping us get settled when we first moved from Germany to Holland, but there was never enough money and never enough food and it was dangerous for us to worship God as we are told in the Bible.

Remember the last time we played together? It was summer and the days were getting longer, and harvest seemed very far away. When you chased me, my shoes got stuck in the peat bog, and we could not pull them out. You were worried that I would need shoes on the great ship that was leaving soon, and you gave me yours. I will never forget that, Willy.

I wore your shoes on the day we boarded the ship. I had only seen ships from a distance, and I always thought they were grand things, very large, and that the men who sailed on them were heroes like we read about in storybooks.

As we walked along the wooden path by the shore, I remember thinking that the boards were so rotten that we might step through them and fall into the sea. Everywhere the gulls were shrieking and crying as if they were laughing at us, taunting us. "Dumplears," I heard them saying, like the people in the town who made fun of us. "Dunkers."

When I looked up at the boat, I thought to myself that it looked so small. Even from the dock it smelled bad, the smell of many people living close together. And the wood of the ship looked every bit as battered and worn as the planks beneath our feet.

Carrying our clothing, furniture, and extra food, we walked up a plank to the deck of the ship, which was rocking back and forth. Mother lost her footing and her packages fell everywhere on the deck. The sailors laughed and did not offer to help, but Father did not answer them, because he believed that we were to abide their abuse meekly and let God settle all things. God is the judge.

Father had warned us that we were never to leave anything out of our sight, that there were thieves and unscrupulous men who would steal all we had, leaving us to starve. I never thought, however, that I would find the sailors to be more dangerous than thieves. They spoke in another language, but you could tell that their words were as foul as the floor of the barnyard back home near Schwarzenau. But Father said we must remember they are all God's children, too.

We climbed down a ladder into the darkness and couldn't see anything at first. It was the foulest pit. I couldn't breathe. I wondered if we were descending into hell. There was the glow of fire in a little stove and smoke that choked us. Many families were already huddled there, some Brethren and some others who also wanted to go to Pennsylvania. They were cooking their own food, as we would do also, except when we had so little that we had to eat what the sailors prepared. I don't know if I can tell you what that was like.

Gradually our eyes got used to things. One family had already taken the cabin with the ladder, so we had to go deeper into the ship. Mother started to cry, and so did my sister, but Father sighed and said when God sent his people to the Promised Land they grumbled aloud and never came to Canaan. Father always tells us stories from the Bible, and so does Mother.

We made up our little room with a bunk and a cook stove. The walls were thin and we could hear everything that happened around us. There were no secrets.

The ship was always moving. Sometimes it moved a little with the waves and people would be sick, and sometimes it moved so much, especially when the storms hit, that we would be very, very sick. It made things smell worse, even though people tried to get on deck before they would vomit. It was very difficult, and no one could eat anything. And even when we felt like eating something, the food was often very bad.

We were not the only Brethren on board. There were others, including Elder John Naas and his family. You remember him. He was so tall that it was difficult for him to squeeze into the dark places. People were often complaining, but not when Brother Naas was there. He always reminded us of where we were traveling and that God was with us.

Everyone looked up to Elder Naas. We had heard stories of how the king's guard tried to force him to serve in their unit, because the king liked very tall men. Some say he was tortured with thumbscrews and with other very painful devices so that he would give in and join the army, but Elder Naas said, "Christ only is my captain," and the king was so impressed that he let him go. But Elder Naas never talked about that. I wish I knew more.

Willy, at first we traveled from Holland to England and were never far from shore, with France on our left and England on our right. We stayed for a time in England to get supplies and to take on extra passengers. There was grumbling, because some said the captain's only thought was to make more money from those who wanted passage. Every corner of the ship was filled. When people started to resent these Englishers, John Naas would remind us that the Apostle Peter said in the Book of Acts that God has no favorites of one people over another, but loves everyone.

Soon we left England behind, and that is when things got very bad, Willy. Day after day, just the sea everywhere. Some days were sunny. Some days there was nothing but the clouds. The boat would rock up and down and back and forth and right and left, and people were always getting sick.

When we tried to eat because we were so hungry, we would then get more sick. There were no medicines, no help for us.

There was water to drink, but it was old water, put into the casks in the Indies, they said, and there were worms in it. Willy, when you get thirsty, you drink it anyway. We cooked with that water, and mother tried to cleanse it, but it was no good. And we kept getting sick.

We had been at sea a week when a woman died. She had wanted to go to Pennsylvania, but she wasn't well, and later she kept saying how sorry she was that she had set out. When she died they wrapped her in a cloth and tied stones to her feet and threw her overboard. My father and the Elder John Naas led us in singing songs to God, but she was not the last one to die on this trip. One man lost his whole family, his wife and his children, one by one. We said more prayers and sang more songs.

Then one day we saw dolphins, which are a sign of good luck. Some of the sailors took a hook that was as big as my hand and pulled in a shark. How that shark fought, thrashing and wriggling in the water. A sailor told us all to stand back. I wasn't afraid but Mother grabbed me and pulled me back. I'm glad she did, because when they pulled that shark onto the deck the whole boat shook. The shark opened its jaws, and if I had been standing near, it could have eaten me in one bite! I screamed, and so did everyone else, but the sailors killed the shark and we all ate of the fish. It had a very odd flavor, but we were glad for the change. It did us much good, and with the change in diet, some seemed to get better.

The worst of it was when the great storm hit. All the sails were taken down, and the ship was tossed about like a leaf upon the river. They tied a sailor (the one who laughed at Mother when she fell on the deck) to the rudder and left him alone to tend to the boat while all the others went below. He was a very brave man and I prayed for him.

The people were very sick and they had no place to go but to be sick in their cabins. It was the worst of all. Everything smelled bad. The babies and even the adults were crying.

But the worst was when they stopped crying, because it meant they had given up hope or had died. Then we would have another funeral at sea, another body weighted down and thrown overboard.

I think it must have been like that for Noah as the waters raged and the heavens opened up. I know our voyage was not as long as his. We had hoped to cross in three months or less, but it stretched to six months.

The Elder John Naas would always give us words of hope. But one day, after the storms were over, he climbed up to the deck in the hour before the sun rose. He did this every day to check the compass, he said, to make sure we were on course. But on that day, like any other, many people were sleeping near that ladder. For some it was a place to get fresh air. Elder Naas was always very careful not to wake people up, because he said they needed to sleep when it was possible.

But that day someone who was sleeping at the foot of the ladder rolled over and knocked the ladder down, and Elder Naas fell from deck level to the floor. He landed on the ladder. I heard it myself and thought it sounded like wood breaking. It was a horrible sound, and it was even worse when Father and I ran over and discovered what had happened.

Oh, Willy, I never felt worse than when I saw him, the one man we all looked up to, lying on the floor, unable to move his legs.

"What will we do?" I asked my father, but there were tears in my father's eyes. That's when I started to give up hope. I wondered if we would ever see land again, if we would all just die at sea, one by one.

But the Elder John Naas quoted from the Psalms: "Bless the Lord, O my soul, and do not forget all his benefits," he said, "…who forgives all your iniquity, who heals all your diseases, who redeems your life from the Pit, who crowns you with steadfast love and mercy, who satisfies you with good as long as you live so that your youth is renewed like the eagle's." He told me it was from Psalm 103. Later I looked it up and read it in the Bible our family brought with us.

If ever we were in the Pit, it was that moment. And for the next two weeks, Elder Naas could not move. But his hope never failed, and he continued to encourage us. Because I had always shown interest, he would send me up on deck to look at the compass for him and to tell him what I saw. Every day I prayed to the Lord that Elder Naas would be healed.

Then one day I came to his cabin and found him sitting up. It was hard for him to move, but he could walk around a little and said that he felt almost as he had before. So the Lord had answered my prayer. We took this as a sign of God's favor.

The next day he could move a little more, and the day after that he climbed the ladder and stood on the deck again. I walked next to him, to help him. I think he liked me. He spoke of his son in Germany, who was an adult and had his own family and had not come over with them.

As we stood together, with the wind blowing and the smell of the sea all around us, an amazing thing happened. Only the day before, we had buried another woman at sea. She had never been well and had always complained about the hardships and that she would not survive the voyage. It was a very sad thing. But on that day, the 17th of September, a bird flew out of the clouds. I will never forget it. It was a yellow water wagtail, like we would see in Germany.

You would have thought it was a long lost friend, the way all the people clapped and cheered. It was as if one of our own, who had already made the journey to Pennsylvania, had come back and found us at sea to tell us that we were nearly there.

"This is like Noah," said the Elder John Naas. "When the dove returned with an olive branch, he knew the Lord had delivered him. The Lord has delivered us!"

The next day a boat came from Rhode Island. It was bound for the West Indies, but their captain took pity on us and sent over some apples. Our own captain took them on board, then gave us one apiece and tossed the rest in the air, one by one, and we scrambled to catch them. I could feel strength returning from the fresh fruit. It was the first fruit I had eaten in months. I have never tasted so sweet an apple.

We lived through another bad storm, and for a time things were terrible indeed, but soon we reached the mouth of the river and headed toward Philadelphia, where we arrived on the 29th.

The Bible says when the Apostle Paul arrived in Rome he was greeted by the brothers and sisters who knew he was coming. Just like Paul, we were greeted by the brethren and the sisters who came out in small boats to bring us bread and apples and peaches and other delicious things. We felt like we were rich. Everyone cried, because we knew this was our new home and that our own people had prepared a place for us.

This is a very beautiful land, Willy, and there is work here for all, and good tillage. We work hard, all of us, but you have never seen such apples.

So much is happening here in our new world. I will be baptized soon. Then I will be able to share the love feast and the washing of the feet and the breaking of communion bread.

The people here work hard at their crafts. There is a man here who is printing Bibles in German. His name is Christopher Sauer. He is not Brethren, but he looks after us and supplies us with Bibles and hymnals and psalters and other good things. He prints the news in German, so we can read it. Our own Bible was much damaged by the trip, but Father says we will soon have one of Sauer's Bibles for our own.

My father says I must finish this letter so it can travel with the other letters being sent back home by the brothers and sisters. Please write to me. And some day if you are able to come with your family, maybe we will see each other again. If not, then God will take care of us both. At night the same moon shines down on us. Let us look at it when it is full and think of each other. God bless you, Willy. I remain

Your friend in Jesus Christ

Jakob Hess

The early Brethren wrote more than one account of the very dangerous crossing from Europe to America. Jakob's letter represents the viewpoint of many who, like John Naas, came to Pennsylvania to claim religious freedom.

3
Bread and Ice

The First Love Feast in America

December 25, 1723

"We're not supposed to cry on Christmas," Magdalena Traut said. She spoke as quietly as possible to Anna Gumre as they sat together while the other Brethren sang hymns and the six new Brethren, who would shortly be baptized, learned Alexander Mack's hymn "Count well the cost."

With those six were seventeen brothers and sisters who had come to Germantown, Pennsylvania, from Germany, bringing with them their Brethren faith and their Brethren practice. They were gathered in the home of Peter Becker, the weaver, who was their leader in this new land.

"I know, I know," Anna sniffled in reply. "It's just that on this holy day I always miss my family the most—and all those people we left behind across the ocean, whom we may never see again."

"Hush, hush," Magdalena scolded. "Now you've got me crying too. We left so many behind to come here."

"On most days life is so busy that there is no time to think about them. Magdalena, I am so happy we came to Germantown. We are free to worship God without being afraid of arrest or imprisonment." Anna daubed her eyes with a handkerchief. "Maybe I just have to get these tears out of my heart before everyone comes to my home later for the love feast."

"That's right!" Magdalena said. "These six new brothers and sisters must know what it means to come together around the table of the Lord! And it does not mean eating burnt food!… Quiet. Don't laugh so loud," she said in response to Anna's giggles. That only made it harder to keep quiet, of course.

Soon Peter Becker rose to take his place at the head of all who were seated in his small, tidy home. Though none of these Brethren were rich, they had enough to eat. So it seemed to Peter Becker to be a good day to put extra wood on the fire to make things warm and bright. Indeed, he could see that some of the men and women were getting a little sleepy from the heat.

"I rise to greet you all in the name of the Lord on this special day when we celebrate his holy birth. I see my friends here, or should I say my brothers and sisters. All of us have traveled by ship to Pennsylvania at great risk to ourselves. Some of us lost all our material goods before we left, because they were taken from us when we insisted that we would worship as the Bible tells us. Some of us lost everything because we spent our inheritance, all that came to us, to support each other in a material way."

As if he were counting heads, Peter named those who had been Brethren in Europe. "I see Johann Heinrich Traut and Jeremiah Traut and Balser Traut, all sack makers. And Magdalena, of course."

Magdalena sat up a little straighter when her name was mentioned, but Brother Becker was still talking. Perhaps he had noticed them talking during the hymns.

"Then there is Heinrich Holtzapfel and Stephen Koch and Jacob Koch. Here is Johannes Hildebrand and his wife, Maria."

Maria smiled at Brother Becker. She had invited him to eat at their house often.

"And there are more. The good farmer Daniel Ritter and George Balzer Gantz with his wife, Johanna; Johannes Preisz and Johannes Kampfer; and, of course, Johannes Gumre and his wife, Anna, who have so graciously offered to host us at the love feast after our worship this morning! Their hospitality is already well known, for they often house our brethren and sisters while they get settled after coming to these shores."

Then he paused. "Some of us lost loved ones on the crossing, who are with God now where they feel no pain. And there are many we left behind, both brothers and sisters in the faith and our earthly families, people who cherished us, or perhaps rejected us when we chose to follow God rather than human wisdom."

He smiled and looked at the two women who were sitting together. "But this is all joy to us; all our trials are joy, at least judging from two of my sisters sitting together at the back who were laughing during our song!

"Some of you know how, this past year, it came to me that we had not gathered since our arrival, all of us together, to celebrate the love feast of our Lord, as Jesus calls us to do in his Holy Word. Four years have gone by, and some have wondered why, especially these six new brothers and sisters in our midst who desire to join us by holy baptism.

"Of course, in part this is because we have been so busy establishing ourselves in our trades, clearing the land for our farms, or caring for our families. We have not been too busy to read our Bibles and to pray alone, or in twos or threes. But we have not all gathered together since we arrived.

"Perhaps also is the fact that when we left Europe we were not all in accord with some of our brothers and sisters who said we must only marry other Brethren, while others of us insisted that scripture allows us to marry others outside our faith and then invite them to join us.

"None of that matters now. When our brothers and sisters asked for baptism, that was a sign for all of us to come together. And this is the day we have selected. Come, rise, let us carry out this command of the Lord."

With that they all rose, the seventeen brothers and sisters, the six newcomers, and the many children who lined the room. They stepped from the Becker house out into a cold December morning. There was snow on the ground, the streets were empty, doors were shut, and windows were latched.

"Where is this place where we will have the baptism?" Anna asked. "I have heard it is not too far from here."

"It's the only real place we could have done this," Magdalena said to Anna. "The sides of the creek are so steep in most places that we can hardly stand on the edge."

Suddenly, there was a racket, with loud, hoarse singing and the banging of metal spoons on pots and lids. A grubby group of mud-smeared men came walking up the lane, hollering. They were wearing dirty, unpatched clothing, with ragged coats. The smell of strong drink wafted before them.

"Try them!" one of them shouted, and they soon surrounded the brothers and sisters.

"La, la, la, la, la, la, la!" they sang, making no sense and banging their pots all the louder. "La, la, la, la, la, la, la!"

"Now sing it!" their leader shouted.

"We want some figgy pudding," they now sang. "We want some figgy pudding, we want some figgy pudding, and a cup of good cheer!"

"And what else?" shouted their leader.

"We won't go until we get some, we won't go until we get some, we won't go until we get some, so bring it right here!"

"Now quick, where's your money? And your drink? This is Christmas!"

Magdalena held tight to Anna. "Oh, it's those Kallithumpian bands again. What a terrible custom they have here in America."

"It should not be allowed," Anna whispered. "What a way to mark Christmas."

"Speak English," the leader said to the women and moved a little closer.

Peter Becker, however, stepped gently in his way. This time he spoke in English, with difficulty, but as clearly as he could manage: "My brother, if there is anything you want, you have simply to ask, and we will give it to you, without the need of threat. But that is true not only for Christmas, but every day. The Lord Jesus has commanded us to feed the hungry, for in the gospel he says whatever we do for the least we do for him."

"Beat him!" shouted one of the ruffians. "Rob him! This is our day. This is when we get our own!"

But the leader was holding up his hand. He looked long and hard at Peter.

"Are you those they call the Dunkers?"

"Yes, we are Brethren, brothers and sisters. Some have called us Dunkers, for that is how we baptize. If you choose to come with us, you may observe how we will baptize in the stream nearby."

"What?" the leader shouted. "But the river is frozen. There is ice. Are you telling me you will break that ice and go into the water?"

"Yes," said Peter simply.

"Then you will die of sickness," sneered the leader.

"The Lord will protect us, as he protected us in our homes in Germany. There we were persecuted for baptizing in this fashion. We will not take sick. Come and see," invited Becker.

"And afterwards, after you freeze yourselves in the river, what will you do next? Set your heads on fire?"

Peter Becker smiled. "No, my brother."

"I'm not your brother! I am an Englishman, and you are a dirty German."

Becker responded, "We are all brothers and sisters in our Lord Jesus Christ. And to answer your question, after we are through, we are going to the home of a brother and sister to share the love feast. We shall wash each other's feet after the manner of Jesus and his disciples, and we shall eat a meal together and share the bread and cup."

"This is too much trouble," groaned one of the ruffians. "Let's beat them and be done with them." And with that he raised a soup ladle to strike Peter Becker.

But the leader pushed him back. "There's no money here, or strong drink. Let us go on our way and find better meat. Farewell, Pastor Dunker. Your church is too hard. Why should I freeze or wash someone's feet? I will let someone be religious for me! Goodbye."

They all breathed a sigh of relief as the ruffians marched away, their singing and banging dying away in the distance.

"How terrible!" Heinrich Holtzapfel said. "Did we flee the persecution of Europe in order to be harassed like this by people who can scarcely claim the title of men?"

"If our brother Alexander Mack were among us," Becker said, "he would tell us to share with them and to recognize in every man and woman a soul that Christ died for. Do not begrudge them this one day that they have to take back money from those who make money off their labor. This was the practice in England, I am told, and they have brought it to America. And remember, when they are poor, they don't have brothers and sisters in Christ, as we do, to take care of them if they should stumble and fall."

"Well," said Anna, "the Lord says if we are true to our beliefs, then we will suffer. That much is sure."

"Oh, no," Magdalena said. "Here come more people."

But the next group was much quieter. A group of four, two men and two women, nicely dressed, walked past the group of Germans.

"Merry Christmas!" one said in English. His nose was bright red, and he had a little trouble staying on his feet. "Merry Christmas! Perhaps we will stop at your house later, Brother Dunker, for a drink."

"Come, come," said the woman who stood next to him. "We have friends to visit, a long list. Let's not waste time with them."

"I don't know which is worse," Magdalena said when they were past. "The poor who bang their pots and take money and drink from the rich, or the rich people who go from house to house all day on Christmas, getting more and more drunk."

"The world is like that, Sister. The world needs the gospel," Peter Becker said.

The group walked carefully down the little roads that made up Germantown, until soon they were beyond the buildings and nearing Wissahickon Creek. At the water's edge, or rather at the edge of the ice, all was still, except for the flutter of a few small birds watching the people and hopping from branch to branch.

At a signal from Peter Becker, the six who were to be baptized knelt down, and he laid his hands on them one by one and prayed aloud. As they all shivered together and huddled close for warmth, he then began to crack the ice with a long stick.

The sound of rushing water greeted them. "See, even in the cold of winter, God's Spirit is bright and alive," Peter said.

Anna watched Peter take a very deep breath and shudder as he stepped into the water. After that he did not hesitate, but walked until the water reached his waist. Quickly, one by one, Martin Urner and his wife, Catherine, and Frederick Lang and John Mayle and Henry Landis with his wife took their turn in the stream while the others on the shore sang Alexander Mack's hymn.

Count well the cost, Christ Jesus said,
When you lay the foundation.
Are you prepared, though all seems lost
To risk your reputation,
Your self, your wealth, for Christ the Lord
As you now give your solemn word?

Within the church's warm embrace
The child of God is molded,
God's Spirit lighting up a face
And by his grace enfolded
And childlike steps by God are led
Into true life these steps are sped.

As quickly as he could, Peter asked the six their baptismal questions and then quickly dunked them three times beneath the water. They sputtered and spluttered in turn, struggling to catch their breath as they were helped to their feet. The others had all taken part in their own time, but that was in the old country. It occurred to Anna as she watched that there was something old about this, like the first Christians who were baptized, and something new, for it was the first Brethren baptism in America—and not illegal!

Quickly they wrapped the newly baptized men and women in layers of warm blankets and walked together back to town, this time to the Gumre home. The lights were bright inside as the winter afternoon began to wane. A roaring fire was waiting for them and, even better, the smell of good food cooking over the fire. There was a large pot of potatoes and carrots and onions and lamb, a delicious smell.

Soon bread, which had been left to rise, was baking in the stone oven. And for those who were too hungry to wait for the feast, there was a bowl of apples, a little dried, but part of the fall's crop and very sweet and hard.

The children began to run around, pretending to baptize the one they caught. Some pretended they were Brother Peter Becker and would act as if they were sharing food with the poor. It was not long before the bowl of apples was empty and more were put out. The children were fed first. They devoured the food on their heaping plates and were promised sweet cake as a reward for waiting quietly and watching the adults as they celebrated the love feast.

Then the adults gathered around the table, with the women on one side of the table and huddled together at the end. The men filled the rest of the spaces, and new members were mixed with the old.

"You will love this," Anna said to Catherine Urner. "This is as close as we can get to Jesus in this life."

They washed feet after Peter Becker read from the Gospel of John, in which Jesus told his disciples to follow his example in serving others in this way so they might be served. A man washed the feet of the man next to him, and that man then washed the feet of the one next to him. The women washed each other's feet on down the line, as well.

Then they served themselves the food. Before they ate, Peter Becker reminded them how Alexander Mack, who still lived back in Europe, had once wondered aloud why others came away hungry from the Lord's Supper, having eaten only a morsel and drunk a drop, when God had called them to a feast! Then reading more from scripture, they ate together.

And finally, as darkness fell outside, those around the table broke the bread together and shared the cup of wine.

Afterwards, with the baptism and the communion over and the sound of the Kallithumpian bands still wandering the street, Anna said, "The food is so good here. Good solid fare, and plenty of it. We did not have this much food in Europe. And we always ate in fear. That makes me wonder why we do not share this blessing with all who live around us. Brother Peter, you said the gospel of Jesus Christ is for all the world. But for the past few years we have been taking care of ourselves, getting used to our new country, and even learning words in English. Is it not time for us to go forth, as the apostles, into all the world to spread the word?"

There was silence for a moment, and then Peter Becker said, "My sister, you are right! Brothers and sisters, let us resolve that when the harvest is over all of us men here present will go forward into the surrounding countryside, planting the more lasting seeds of the gospel."

"Just the men?" asked Magdalena.

"Well, yes," he said. "And you women will run the farms, as you do so well, with the children and whatever help we can find. We will return before the winter turns evil! What a harvest it will be, not only from the goodness of the earth, abundance more than we can imagine, but also a harvest for the Lord of souls who need his love!"

Later Magdalena stopped Anna as they were both preparing to leave with their families.

"Do you still feel like crying?" she asked.

"A little," said Anna. "I still miss my family so far away. But I know now that it is like the gospel story we read together, where the people told our Lord Jesus that his mother and his brothers were waiting for him outside. And he said that his real family included all who did the will of the Heavenly Father."

She smiled at Magdalena. "This is my family. The others, so far away, will always be precious to me. But this is my home, this is my family, all of you brothers and sisters who have taken up the yoke of the gospel and walk together in love."

❦

The next year the Fourteen Evangelists, as they came to be known, traveled out from Germantown and founded new churches at Conestoga and beyond. All the Brethren churches that exist now have come about because these men set out in the name of the Lord.

4
Lost and Found

Alexander (Sander) Mack, Jr.

1745

Sander Mack was tired of
running away. He stood
outside his little hut, built
like those of his compan-
ions who had sought soli-
tude in order to study the
Bible and grow closer to
God, to grow their gardens and to catch game and feed

each other. He stood there in the sun, knowing that summer would soon be over and that the fall's bite and winter's chill would soon be setting in. Sander Mack just wanted to go home.

But Sander wasn't sure what home was, or if he had a
home to go back to. Nor was he even sure who he was. Those
whose huts were built near his own didn't call him Alexander
or Sander or Mack. They called him Timotheos. And though
their names were Israel, Samuel, and Gabriel Eckerlin, they
called each other Onesimus, Jephune, and Jotham.

They were all running away, Sander realized, and they were all running away from running away.

Sad, sad, sad. Sander knew he was very sad. Inside his hut, with its simple bed, he had left the Bible open, but every time he opened the pages and read the words he thought of his father, Alexander Mack, and the way he would preach. Every word about the Heavenly Father spoke to him about his earthly father.

And now his father was dead. He had been dead for ten years.

When Sander was born, his name was Alexander Mack, Jr., but soon everyone called him Sander Mack. His father had been the first minister of the Brethren. The younger Mack's nickname was Sander so people wouldn't confuse the two of them. He had been proud to bear his father's name when they were pursued from place to place by those who persecuted the Brethren in Europe and on that day in 1728 when he himself had chosen to be baptized. He was sixteen when his father finally said he was old enough. It was a great day, coming up out of the water as a new person in Christ and as the son of such a great man he was proud to call his father.

But life was still hard. His mother and his baby sister had died a few years before when sickness swept their village. All of their money had been spent helping to support the other brothers and sisters who lost everything when they chose to be baptized and become part of the Brethren. How sad that had been. But he and his father had each other, and somehow, with their faith in God, they had come through that awful time.

In 1729 the two of them set out for America. The trip seemed to take forever, but they knew there was a new life on the other shore. And more than that, they would be joining their brothers and sisters who had already gone before, and his father would become the minister of the whole church, united once again. Stepping onto the shore in Philadelphia, his legs had been wobbly after the long voyage, but he had been proud to tell the man who took down their names that he was the son of Alexander Mack. Of course, the dock official didn't seem to know there was anything exceptional about his father, but everyone else did, and they were treated very special.

Sander thought of what his father had hoped to do, how he had been welcomed and had become the minister of the Brethren in America—but also how he could not bring the people back together.

There was a man named Conrad Beissel who said God spoke to him, and many people believed it. Many of the brothers and sisters left the Brethren and came to live at Ephrata, where Conrad Beissel was the superintendent. There they sang the songs of angels and worked hard all day and served God and not people.

Sander's father had hoped to heal the break between the Brethren and Conrad Beissel, but it had not been possible. Beissel always denied Mack's authority, always refused to listen to anyone else. Sander knew it had broken his father's heart to see the Brethren torn in two, and it was one of the reasons his father had died at the age of 55—much too soon.

The younger Alexander Mack always thought of his father, and the thoughts would often bring Sander back to the day when his father was buried. There had been the simple wooden box. Everyone cried and everyone sang. After that, people would look in on Sander, cooking for him and caring for him while they waited for him to get over the loss.

But he couldn't. He was always sad.

Then Conrad Beissel himself, of all people, invited Sander to come to visit his cloister in Ephrata. Sander felt suspicious when the invitation came, but something led him on. Perhaps he hoped to fill the empty spot in his life. Maybe Conrad Beissel would be like a father to him. When he saw the man, he was struck by how deep his eyes were, and how soothing his voice, and how everyone around him seemed anxious to please him.

Sander thought back to the first time he had walked around the Ephrata Cloister. People in their robes were working hard, smiling, eating together. They hardly ever slept, and when they did, it was on wooden planks with wooden pillows. They worshiped several times during the day and were awakened to worship again in the middle of the night. Every hour, every second, was spent in a rhythm that was out of step with the world, but meant to be in harmony with God's will.

And harmony was the word for their singing as well. The Brethren had always enjoyed singing. The brothers who slept in prison and worked in hard labor at Solingen had written many hymns and found comfort in singing. The brothers and sisters sang on the ships that sailed across the ocean. Worship was always filled with singing. His father had led the singing on many occasions and had written hymns himself.

But nothing like this. Sander really enjoyed his visit to the cloister. Even after he went home, their singing was still ringing in his ears. After a matter of days, he returned, asking to be allowed to stay. Perhaps the work, the singing, the prayer, and very little sleep would leave him no time for sadness. Perhaps finally he could become a new person and leave the sorrow behind.

For a while everything was good. Sander didn't want to say his father had been wrong, but it seemed Superintendent Beissel was right about a lot of things. The superintendent gave him a new name, Timotheus, after the young companion of the Apostle Paul, and in that name Sander felt that he had finally found a new life.

But then, even there in the cloister, people showed their bad side. Every time a brother or sister had a good idea, or wrote a song, or shared some thought about the scripture, Beissel would grow—well—if not angry, then different. Maybe jealous.

This was especially true regarding Sander's friend Israel Eckerlin, who was given the name Onesimus. Israel was the prior, second in command to the superintendent, and he saw to the building of new quarters. He planted trees, thought of new ways to grow food better, more plentifully, and Israel sang his own songs and many others. People turned to him.

Sander liked him too. He got the idea, however, that Superintendent Beissel didn't like it when Sander praised an idea from Onesimus.

When Onesimus left on a journey, the superintendent tore down the buildings, cut down the trees, and burned the hymns on the fire. That made Sander wonder. Could anyone, even the superintendent, be right about everything? Why did Beissel think he had to be right all the time? Why was he jealous of others?

Superintendent Beissel had warned them that they were putting too much of themselves, too much of their humanity, into their possessions. He told them he had to burn their things so they would not become too proud. It was a bitter thing to hear, but they wondered if perhaps he was right.

Sander and the Eckerlin boys decided to take a trip to the north and east, to the colonies of New England, to preach the gospel and to see if time away would make things better. But when they returned, it was obvious that Beissel had turned the minds of the others against them. No one would talk with them or eat with them or pray with them. No one sang their songs.

Sander felt sad all over again, only worse. He had hoped to escape the sadness, but things were worse. He decided it was time to walk away—from Ephrata and from the sadness.

Together Sander and the Eckerlins walked south and west into Virginia. They traveled four hundred miles on foot, following the rivers, walking old Indian paths across the mountains, foraging for food, walking until they were so tired that they would fall asleep immediately. Sander didn't want to think. He didn't want to dream. He just wanted to forget. He wanted to forget about his father, about Beissel, about the brothers and sisters among the Brethren, and about his brothers and sisters in the cloister.

The men eventually stopped near a pioneer settlement called Strasburg. It was a rough place where the people were carving out a new life in the wilderness. Sander and his friends built huts, cleared the land, grew crops, read their Bibles, and prayed.

But there was still too much time to think.

Sander couldn't forget about the Brethren he had left behind. He had heard that some of them were arguing about the way to hold the love feast. Some said the feetwashing should come first, and others said it should come after the meal. Some were also saying that one man should wash the feet of the man next to him, and that man should wash the feet of the man next to him, and so with the women as well. Others said no, two men should wash the feet of all the men, and two women should wash the feet of all the women. Both sides were pointing to their Bibles and saying they were right. And he heard that some of them were not speaking to each other.

It all reminded him too much of the time in Germany when some of the Brethren had said one could marry outside the church, and others said you could only marry someone in the church. Both sides pointed to their Bibles and insisted they were right. And for a time both sides had gone their separate ways.

He knew this was not right. He knew the brothers and sisters would take in total strangers and give them food and clothing and help them on their way. He knew the brothers and sisters were always there to help rebuild a barn destroyed by fire, no matter if the owner was a member of the church or not. But within the church there was argument and jealousy.

That's why the Brethren had to keep getting together—to remind themselves of how much they loved each other and needed each other. They needed to remember that the love of Jesus came first, and all of their concerns came second, and that even if they disagreed, one side could give in to another in love.

Yes, Sander thought. That's why it was so important to meet together when necessary, at least every year. And as the brothers and sisters headed west, farther and farther away, looking for land, this would be a way of keeping the Brethren together in one body, caring for each other, sending alms if needed, and sharing out of their plenty to those in need. It would be a time for preaching and studying the Bible.

Suddenly it was if Sander could smell the love feast, the lamb and the potatoes and the carrots and the apples and peaches and other fruit. Now he realized that Superintendent Beissel had not allowed his own people to eat much, but in the New Testament, God's people were always coming together in their love feasts, in their meals, sharing out of what they had.

There shouldn't have to be one strong leader who did all the thinking and made all the decisions for everyone else. Everyone had something to share. Everyone had a song to sing. Everyone in their baptism should be able to read from their Bibles and share their wisdom.

Sander walked back into his hut and picked up the Bible that was lying on the bed. He turned to the passage he had been reading in the Book of Acts, where Philip was led by the

Spirit to the Gaza Road and spoke to an Ethiopian in a chariot who had been reading the Book of Isaiah. In the text Philip asked the Ethiopian if he understood what he was reading.

Suddenly the answer given by the Ethiopian made perfect sense, almost as if God were talking to Sander directly: "How can I know unless someone explains it to me?" And how could the Brethren know, how could the brothers and sisters know, unless someone explained to them how to come together in love, to disagree in love, to meet together to settle things, but also just to gather together in worship and praise? How could they know unless someone told them?

Who could tell them? Surely not he himself! He had turned his back on them. Wouldn't they resent him? How could they ever accept him back?

The sun slowly set, the green of the hills turned to gray, and finally all was black, except for those shadows that came from the setting moon. The stars wheeled around the heavens, the Big Dipper circling the Little Dipper as Sander remembered the words his father had written in his Bible about the great size of the sun and Jupiter, and about the tremendous distance of Mercury from the Earth. "Oh what a wonderfully great and incomprehensible Creator must he be who has created and sustained such creations! God has thus placed us in this world as in a foreign garden, in which we are to live and to eat all of its fruits, but we are not allowed to take anything away with us. Rather, we must leave everything in the world just as God commanded!"

Oh, how is the time so urgent, Sander thought, that God gives us only once. And he began to hum, and then sing that hymn:

Oh, how is the time so urgent
Which God gives us only once;
And how is the world so empty,
Which by man is loved too much!

The time is urgent, he thought to himself. Someone must save the brothers and sisters. Someone must remind them of how wonderfully great the Creator is and how petty our disagreements!

Then Sander fell asleep, and toward dawn he seemed to dream about the corn, soon to be harvested. Yet in his dream he saw Indians come and lay waste to the corn.

Sander awoke, startled. What did the dream mean? He knew that many Indians were friendly, but that others were resentful for losing their land and attacked the settlers.

At their meal together, Sander told the others about his dream and asked what they thought it meant. They could give him no reply. But a few days later Indians did come in the night and destroyed the corn. When Sander awoke and discovered what had happened, he took it as a sign that finally he was to return to the Brethren.

Yes! Now he was certain. It was in the love feast that he could be close to Jesus, washing the feet of his brothers and sisters. It was in the love feast he could be close again to his father and mother, until God called him to his heavenly home.

"I don't want to be Timotheus anymore," he said aloud. "I want to be Sander Mack!"

His companions were skeptical, but Sander urgently believed that God was calling him, that God had spoken

to him through the Bible, and that the dream had been
a confirmation.

"We all lose someone," he told his companions. "I know
that now. But we always have Jesus. Jesus said he would be
with us always, even unto the end of the age. And we
always have God's people to be with us as well."

It was a long walk back, four hundred miles and more,
once again on foot, with his pack and his Bible and almost
no belongings. And all the way back Sander thought to himself that if the brothers and sisters would accept his apology,
he would not put himself forward, but if they asked, he
would serve them faithfully all his days.

"And may God grant my days are long, not for myself,
but for service."

Sander realized he should never have left the Brethren,
where he was needed. He should have shared his sorrow, his
sadness, and allowed them to pray with him and for him, to
walk with him through the valley of the shadow of death.

"For I am with you," a voice seemed to say.

"I know," Sander said aloud.

Weeks later he was back in Germantown, walking down
the familiar streets. He was afraid to meet the eyes of those
he knew. Surely they were angry at him for leaving them so
many years before. He thought they would turn away and
ignore him, shun him, for the sin of leaving them behind.

But the brothers and sisters recognized him, and he was
embraced by those who had missed him. The word spread
quickly that he was back, and he was given new clothes and
a place to live. The brothers and sisters prepared a love feast
to celebrate his return.

"Welcome home!" they told him. "We missed you! We are so glad you are back!"

"I am Sander Mack," he said to them. "I am Alexander Mack, Jr., and I have come to serve God's people however you should see fit."

"Welcome home," they said to him. "Welcome home."

Sander Mack lived ninety-one years and helped to counsel his brothers and sisters in their trials and tribulations. He wrote many poems and hymns, as well as the first Brethren histories. Thanks to him much that might have been lost was saved. Sander worked hard to keep the Brethren together, to help them get past their differences and to see how God had called them all into one family.

Some of the Eckerlins were kidnapped years later by French and Indian soldiers. Their fate is uncertain, but after cruel mistreatment, it is said they died as prisoners in the hands of the French.

5
Angels in Pennsylvania?

Catharine Hummer

May 28, 1763, Conestoga, Pennsylvania
"Whoever heard of a woman preaching?" Peter Dierdorf asked. He was the miller of his village. Like all the other Brethren present, he had come to Annual Meeting here at the Conestoga meetinghouse to hear about this strange thing and to talk about the teenaged girl named Catharine Hummer, who saw angels—who *said* she saw angels.

"And she is not even a woman," Jakob Meyer replied. "She is only a girl. A young girl."

"How can it be," Henry Neff added, "that an angel might choose to speak with her but not to any of us, who have faithfully served God here in the world, tending to the fields so that God in his wisdom might reap a harvest of souls?"

"Well…," said Christopher Sauer II. Whenever he started to speak, the others would pause to listen. His father had printed the first Bibles in America in Germantown and had been sympathetic to the Brethren. Christopher Sauer II had joined the Brethren Church, built upon his father's business, and printed the Bible again. He was a very rich man and the benefactor of many who were poor.

"Well," he continued, "I recall how in the letter to the Hebrews the Apostle Paul tells us that God spoke to the people in various ways. And in these latter days, we often hear of those who speak in strange tongues or tell of angelic visits, repeating revelations they have received that they suppose came from God's Holy Spirit. Why should God not speak as he chooses, whether through one of us elders of the church, or through a young girl? The wisdom of this world is folly; perhaps God has chosen to speak through the weak to demonstrate his strength."

"I will never believe God has spoken through Catharine Hummer," spoke Nicholas Lettermann with some heat. "I say it is the familiar spirit from below the earth. And I think that her father, Peter Hummer,…"

"Peter Hummer is a respected minister," interrupted Alexander Mack, Jr, "who is worthy at least that we should listen to him and his daughter. And that is why we are having this meeting. Many times in the past when we Brethren have disagreed it has led to division and strife. Now we should listen to each other with love and respect, for we are all brothers and sisters in Jesus Christ. I ask you to withhold judgment until we have heard our brother and sister and have had time to talk together in love about this matter. Never again should we break apart because we disagree."

"Never say never," muttered Matthew Schweitzer, but the others did not hear him.

Twenty-two bearded men took their seats. An older man, with a black broad-brimmed hat, and a teenaged girl in a black bonnet walked into the room. This was Peter Hummer and his daughter Catharine.

At first Catharine wondered if this was how the council known as the Sanhedrin had looked to Jesus when he was on trial before them. But no, Sander Mack, who had spoken to her earlier, was smiling and nodding to her in encouragement.

Sander Mack stood up and said: "I welcome you, and I welcome also all who are here to represent the Brethren. We have come together in fellowship and love—to pray, to worship, and also to hear about this new thing."

Catharine's father spoke first. Peter Hummer was the first minister of White Oak and one of the first settlers only a few years before. Catharine had many older brothers and sisters, but she always suspected she was her father's favorite. She had grown up listening to him preach and was sure that his was the face and voice of an angel…until, of course, she had actually met an angel.

"Listen," said Peter Hummer. "In the prophet Joel, it says in those days that God will pour out his Spirit on all and that the young men will see visions and the young girls will dream dreams. This was spoken of by the prophet. And it says also in the Bible that there is a river that makes glad the

people of God. My daughter Catharine has come to tell us of
that river! What she says is a true thing, and many others
have testified to seeing angels as well. We have traveled as
far as sixty miles, a three-day walk, to tell people of this great
thing that has happened. She has seen angels. We should be
listening, not criticizing, as some of you are doing. You say
that no girl could see angels. You speak against her character.
You know nothing! It is as Solomon wrote in his song, 'Do
not gaze at me because I am dark, because the sun has gazed
on me. My mother's sons were angry with me; they made me
keeper of the vineyards, but my own vineyard I have not
kept!' By that I mean that I am browned by labor and have
ignored my own farm work in order to do God's work. Your
scorn is my reward for doing the Lord's labor!"

"Please," Sander Mack said, rising again to soothe the
broad-shouldered man. "Do not bring too much of the
human into this. We wish to hear not what others say, but
what it is your daughter has seen. Angels in Pennsylvania.
Please, Catharine, tell us more."

But Jacob Stutzmann laughed. "Angels in Pennsylvania?
Who has heard of such a thing?"

Catharine smiled shyly, and all grew silent. But she did
not speak at first. Instead, she sang.

There are angels in the corn field.
There are angels in the barn, up in the air.
There are angels waiting to be born, dear.
There are angels, children, angels everywhere.

Then she spoke:

> *While growing up, I've always heard the Old*
> *Brethren tell about riding to the New World on the*
> *wings of the wind. I have never been to the Old World.*
> *For me this is the only world, until the next world, the*
> *real world. I want to tell you about that real world and*
> *how it was revealed to me by the angels. For the time*
> *grows short and soon all will be weighed in the balance.*
>
> *The Old Brethren always talk about the way the sky*
> *stood still when they were on the boat, but the sea itself*
> *rolled up and down. Whether it was day or night, the*
> *sky stood still, they said. And beneath their feet, the*
> *ship was always rolling.*
>
> *That was how it felt when the angel came to visit me.*
> *The angel was still, attached to the unmoving circles of*
> *heaven, standing in eternity, but I suddenly became*
> *aware how the pleasant earth, the ground beneath my feet,*
> *seemed suddenly to be moving up and down, right and*
> *left, all around.*
>
> *Mother has said there is too much music in me. Oh,*
> *how we Brethren raise our voices in song. We do not*
> *use the vain instruments of the worldly churches, but*
> *sing only. But when the angel sang to me, there was*
> *more than a voice, also timbrel and the beating and the*
> *pounding of waves and the blowing of winds and the*
> *growing of grass and the passing of kings and suns.*
>
> *There are angels in the corn*
> *There are angels who can hover in the air*
> *There are angels dancing on the morn*
> *There are angels, children, angels everywhere.*

For a moment Catharine stopped and closed her eyes, almost as if she had faltered and could talk no longer.

"More, more!" her father said quietly.

Catharine kept her eyes closed tightly, and she was shaking, as if the memory were too much, but she began again to speak.

> *Earlier in the day I was milking the cows. I stood for a moment in the fields and smelled the wind. It was October, but it no longer smelled like October. The west wind brought rain and the south wind brought summer. Northern blasts stripped the limbs of their leaves. The occasional eastern breeze carried upon it the smell of the city far away, like when we make the trip to market in Germantown in the spring and in the autumn.*

> *This wind seemed to come from all around. No October wind should be this warm. Were these the smells of the Caribees, the distant lands that only poets know? Was this a world that never knew wheat nor waves of rye and harvest? What fruits on boughs unguessed were dropping to the loamy earth to seed?*

> *No. It smelled too homely, of buckwheat pancakes and spicy sausage, smokehouses and filled barns. Of untold bounty and fulfilled harvests.*

> *Only warm wasn't the word, for I still felt the chill against my arms. Then I saw the angel.*

She paused.

> *How might I describe the angel's face? That there were eyes of a sort, though not human eyes? A mouth,*

yes, the angel had a mouth because the angel spoke. A nose? I never thought to look. Hair? It might have been hair or it might have been glory. The angel's face was what it was, and not something else entirely.

The size was another matter. Bigger than the valley and smaller than a nutshell. But mostly not of this place, both so near and far away. It was not touching this earth, I would say, for it seemed to be in a different place altogether, a bigger place, on which it struggled to keep its balance. It was all it could do to stand still upon this solid earth while watching for obstacles some- place else, that real place where it resided.

As for the rest, it is easy to describe. The prophet saw the six wings and the six arms folded over the chest and the waist and the legs, and I saw the same thing, and then there was the robe, which would have seemed so white were it not for the brightness of the face.

Yet there was a clear separation between earth and angel. Not a blade of grass, not a clod of dirt, was bent by its touch.

"Rise," said the angel, a thundering voice towering above me. "Do not bend to worship me."

Then the angel, small and floating only inches from my ear, whispered, "Rise, for, like you, I am a servant of the only One worthy of worship."

No one spoke or made a sound as Catharine continued. The grown men, who had insisted they would never listen to a woman preacher, could not move.

*The moon was nearly full and it was high in the sky.
It should have been the brightest object in the night,
drowning out the Milky Way and the stars. But now
even the full moon seemed pale, and the heavens seemed
no longer appropriate for the kingdom of the air.*

*Normally I would have expected moonshadows, cast
from the tree in all directions as the king of night rested
overhead. Oh, they were there, but dim against the dark
shadows cast in the wake of the angel. Even so, I knew
it had to be late from the height of the moon.*

*"Yes, my friend," the angel said. "It is midnight and
late. The hour of midnight is approaching."*

Then I asked, "Who are you?"

"My name is Wonderful," the angel replied.

*"Then you are the one who visited Manoah's wife," I
said. "You told her she would give birth to Samson.
What have you come to say?"*

*"Alas, what shall I say," the angel replied, as it
seemed to shrink, even as its concern shrank from the
ordering of the heavens to the ordering of human souls.
"Love has grown cool among the Brethren. Oh, that this
were not so among those who are Brethren in the faith!"*

*I knew this was the love of a scarred back, torn by
splinters, the love of a forehead pierced by thorns, the
love of hands and feet cut by nails, the love of a body
scored by wounds. This was the love that created summer breezes and howling winter winds, the love that
called the corn from the soil, a love whose no meant yes
to life for many.*

I am well, I thought to myself, and have never felt so much at peace. "I am well," I said aloud.

And the angel began to sing, "How very well I feel! How very well I feel! When our God doth show himself in spirit to my soul…"

"Sing with me," the angel commanded, and I sang these words as though I had studied them all my life.

So that within I leap and jump for joy
And bring all praise and honor to the Lord, although
*   the tongue oft silence keeps.*
The children of God indeed sow
In sorrow and in tears.
But at last the year yieldeth what they long for.
For the time of harvest cometh
When they gather the sheaves
And all their grief and pain is turned to pure joy and
*   laughter!*

I asked if I might go wake my friends, but the angel said that all my friends were asleep and their hearts also want to sleep. This caused me to weep, but the angel caused me to sing even more and told me to weep no more. And then the angel took me into the highest heaven. And I saw that there is a great water that runs from Noon between Morning and Midnight, dividing the earthly from the eternal realm. When a man dies and leaves this earthly realm, he imagines himself alive and does not know anything of his having died, and yet he finds himself a stranger on earth. Then he comes to a

great road that leads from Evening toward Morning; after
he has traveled some distance on this road, a broad road
branches off to the left, leading to damnation and hell.

The road ascends a little until it reaches a certain
height, when it suddenly descends, and there hundreds
on hundreds are traveling. But on the road that leads
toward Morning, sixties on sixties are traveling. This
road leads to the water mentioned, but the other one,
almost directly toward Noon, brings you to the water
sooner. On this road none but adults walk toward the
temple of Mount Zion.

Then the angel said: "And then the Lord will say:
'Come ye pious and baptized, who have persevered to
the end, come over here; come you who are baptized and
have persevered to the end.' "

And then I saw that many who would cross were not
baptized in this life and must be baptized.

"I've heard enough," said Henry Neff, crossing his arms.
"As the tree falls, so it lies. We accept the gospel in this life
or we are lost forever."

"Yet our ancient ancestor Alexander Mack wrote something of the same sort," Christopher Sauer pointed out. "He
wrote about how the punishments of a wrathful God are terrible, but that they may not last forever. Remember his
works that I printed recently?"

"But there is more you do not mention, Catharine," Peter
Dierdorf said suspiciously. "It is said that you cannot see these
angels unless you are left alone in a room with Sebastian

Keller. This Keller is an unmarried man. It is not right that you should be left alone with an unmarried man. I say these stories of angels are meant to mask your sinful behavior."

"I know this Keller," Sander Mack interrupted, even as Peter Hummer rose angrily. Catharine Hummer gazed serenely at Dierdorf, as one unashamed.

"This Keller and I lived together at the cloister of Conrad Beissel many years ago," Mack continued. "I know him to be an honorable and godly man. He has been married before, and that wife, a godly woman, died in childbirth. To accuse Keller is to accuse me, for the two of us have walked far in our spiritual journey together—from the Brethren to be with Beissel, and after a time of repentance, we came back to the Brethren. So, let whoever is without sin cast the first stone."

"Please," Catharine said, "let me say one thing more. Glory to God in the highest for his great love, kindness, and mercy, for he does not forsake those who believe in him, but awakens them from the indolence of the world and from their lusts and desires.

"Dear Brother Sander Mack! I thank you warmly for your love and loving admonitions and for your warm greeting. I, Catherine Hummer, your lowliest fellow-sister, will be patient in the paths of tribulation, for the dear Savior has said that one must pass through many tribulations to enter the kingdom of God. Therefore, I will prepare myself for it as far as the Lord provides grace that I might be found worthy to enter into the kingdom of God, for the winter of persecution is here.

"Contempt and persecution are great, but I comfort myself with the dear Savior and with the small herd of Zion, which has been gathered from all peoples. I am not only persecuted by the world but also hated by those who call themselves believers. They say that what has happened through me is idolatry. They blaspheme about something that they know nothing about. May the Lord have mercy on them and not punish them according to their merits.

"Dear Brother Sander, you once said that, in the end, the weightiest will weigh less than nothing, once they are weighed on the right scales. I am indeed imperfect, but may the Lord put his good spirit into my heart so that when I am weighed, I might have the correct weight and be taken out of this sorrowful world into eternal rest, where no enemy can trouble me any more.

"I firmly believe that the day of the Lord is much nearer than is believed. Dear brothers, I am saying this in great meekness and imperfection. I hope, however, you will not reject what I say but rather consider it and hear it in love. Whenever and wherever I may have erred, I will gladly be reminded of it by you and accept it from you in love."

The Brethren met for a time and discussed this and decided that they would not seek division, but would listen to each other in love. They said that Peter Hummer should repent of any harsh words he had spoken to those who criticized his daughter and that all rumors and harsh expressions should be abandoned.

They agreed they could come to no agreement about the occurrence in question, but begged instead for those on both sides of the controversy not to judge each other, but to receive one another in the love and unity of Christ.

Catharine later married Sebastian Keller, and they went on to have a family in due season. She no longer saw angels.

6
A Clear Conscience

Christopher Sauer II

July 27, 1778, Germantown, Pennsylvania

Christopher Sauer II sat at the
table and tried to catch his
breath. He had only been home a
few days, and his life had
become very difficult.

The war between the colonies
and the British meant that people had to choose sides—and
that wasn't easy because of the
way both sides treated people.
But recently things had become
even more dangerous.

He took a deep breath. He was fifty-seven years old and
overweight. It was getting harder and harder to get around.
He was really feeling his age, especially after what had happened to him just two months ago.

As always when he was upset, Christopher Sauer II
opened the Bible that he kept on the table. This was not just

any Bible. This German Bible had been printed by his father, Christopher Sauer I, after whom he was named. It was the first Bible of its kind printed in America in 1743. It had taken a long time to complete, and he had helped his father work on it when he wasn't busy on some of the many other things they produced at the print shop. Even though this was God's Word, Christopher always felt as if it was also the family's Bible, because they had printed it. And that's what other people called it as well—the Sauer Bible.

Having Bibles printed in Germantown meant that more people could afford to own their own Bible, because they didn't have to pay lots of money to have Bibles sent from across the ocean.

Christopher was three years old when he came to America with his father, who taught him that other people mattered. He had seen his father care for the German-speaking immigrants when they arrived, taking them into the Sauer home and helping them get settled on their own land or in their own trade.

His father had always admired the Brethren and had printed many things for them. When Christopher grew old enough, he joined the Brethren church himself. As time passed he took over the printing business and made it grow, so that now there were both a print shop and a paper mill. He also made his own ink and his own type.

Christopher printed hymn books and sermon books and books about education. He also printed a popular almanac, which told about the rising and setting of the sun and moon, about the seasons for planting and harvesting, and included many helpful facts about raising crops and taking care of soils. They were printed in both German and English, so that all people could learn and sing and pray.

Christopher Sauer II had two sons and named the first son Christopher Sauer III. For a time all was well with the world. Until recently, that is, with this terrible war between the colonies and the British. Like many German-speaking people, Christopher Sauer found it hard to hate the British, because they had given his people the freedom to come to Pennsylvania to practice their faith without persecution.

Now he looked at the pages of his Bible, turning as he often did to the Psalms. There, in the 23rd Psalm he read, "Though I walk in the valley of the shadow of death, I will fear no evil, for you are with me." Christopher Sauer II prayed a little prayer and asked God to be with him, no matter what happened next.

With that, there was a pounding at the door. Christopher struggled to his feet. He again thought of that night, just two months ago, when there had been a pounding at his door. Surely not again. He had been promised he'd be safe when he returned to Germantown.

Christopher opened the door. This time it wasn't a band of ruffians dressed in masks with torches and ropes, like it had been before. There were two military officers, dressed in the uniforms of the Continental Army. But he still felt the same dread.

"My name is Colonel Smith," said one. "And this is Colonel Thompson. May we come in?"

"Yes, yes, of course," Christopher said. "What can I do for you?"

"Well, sir, we have come to ask you if you have posted special bail at the supreme court in Lancaster," Colonel Smith said. He was very polite.

"On the charge of being a traitor," snarled Colonel Thompson, as he looked at Christopher Sauer II suspiciously.

"But I am not a traitor," Christopher protested. "I live here. I work here. That is my shop next door. Everyone knows me here as an honest man."

"Perhaps," Colonel Smith said very smoothly. "Honest you may be, but loyal is another matter. Do you not know that while you were away in May there was a charge of treason brought against you and your family, treason against the Continental Congress? You failed to answer the summons and you and your family were found guilty. Since you never posted bail, we have come to inventory all you own—lock, stock, and barrel—so that it can be sold at auction to support the Continental Congress. Are you telling me you never heard of this?"

For a moment Christopher was unable to speak.

"But we are Brethren. We do not serve a king or a congress. Jesus Christ is our Lord."

"Well," Colonel Thompson snarled, "you can still serve Jesus Christ when you see him, but around here the Continental Congress is king, see? And this here piece of paper says you're a traitor, and we're to sell everything at auction to pay for your crime."

"Perhaps you should sit down, sir," Colonel Smith said. "You don't seem well."

"Yes, yes. I will sit down," Christopher answered. "Listen, yes, I heard something about the charges, but I have come back to take care of it."

"And what kept you so long?" sneered Colonel Thompson.

"I was held by you Americans after my—after what they did to me. They wouldn't let me come back here. How could I answer charges that I was not a traitor when your government prevented me from coming back?"

"That's not our problem," Colonel Thompson answered. "This here's a piece of paper and it says what it says. It says you are a traitor. All you Germans are traitors!"

"I am Brethren," Christopher Sauer protested. "We serve God, and not any government."

"But many of you seem much more comfortable with the British than with us," Colonel Smith noted.

"Some of us are not disloyal to the crown, that is true, Christopher admitted. "But remember, we could not practice our faith in the old country. Shouldn't we be grateful to those who gave us the freedom to practice our faith?"

"But this isn't about faith. This is about taxes," Colonel Thompson argued. "We don't want to pay taxes to a government that is so far away without representation. And what do you think about paying your taxes?"

"The Bible tells us to be good citizens. We pay our taxes to the British. And we Brethren are also the first to pay our taxes to your Continental Congress. Can you patriots say the same? Have you paid your taxes to your own government?"

"We're wasting our time," Colonel Thompson declared.

"But ask my neighbors!" Christopher Sauer protested. "Our family serves everyone. English printing, German printing. All are God's children."

"How can I ask your neighbors? They all speak German, and I don't," sneered Colonel Thompson.

"Don't you know what my father did—what I am doing?" asked Christopher. "He printed the first Bible here in America that was written in a European tongue. Every other Bible is imported across the ocean. But this is an American Bible." He pointed to the book. "Look how beautiful this is. It's the Holy Word of God! And it is printed on American paper made from American trees, bound in American leather."

"How can it be an American Bible if it is written in German?"

"We Germans are part of America too. This land has many different people in it. The Indians? They are Americans, and I have said so in my paper and demanded better treatment for them. The African slaves? They are Americans, too, and must be freed. I have written that in my paper, too."

"But your paper is in German."

"And we also print many materials in English. Didn't you learn your catechism when you were little? We printed the catechism in English and in German for everyone." Christopher reminded them.

"Well, speaking of that," Colonel Smith said smoothly, "you also print newspapers that seem to favor the British."

"Isn't freedom of the press one of the things you are fighting for?"

"Yes, but not freedom for those who disagree with us! Listen, Sauer. You are a wealthy man. You have grown rich in this country, and now you are found to be a traitor to this country. If you disagree, you can have a hearing to contest this."

"When?"

"After the sale is over." The two men were not sympathetic.

Christopher Sauer took another deep breath and sat back in his chair. Then he spoke: "Let me ask you a question. What is the penalty for treason?"

"Hanging," Colonel Smith said.

"But they did not hang me. After they mistreated me, they let me go—and that was two months ago. You and your comrades were so brave that you came in the night without warning, so brave that many of you would fight an old man." Christopher Sauer paused. It was not right to be so angry. The Bible said God's people would be persecuted, and that they must bear it patiently. But persecution was always something that happened to people in the past. Now it was happening to him. Still, if the Apostle Paul could testify without fear before Felix the Governor, then he would state his case as well.

"I was here at my home on the 24th of May when men from Captain McClean's company surrounded my house and took me from my bed in the dark of night, so I suppose they felt safe. They tied me up, a sick old man, and dragged me through the Indian corn. When I could not move fast enough, they struck me in the back with their bayonets. They made me a prisoner in the barn of a local farmer, Bastian Miller, and when morning came they…"

Christopher Sauer found it hard to continue, but Colonel Smith encouraged him.

"They stripped me naked to the skin and gave me an old shirt and breeches so torn that I could hardly cover my nakedness. Then they cut off my beard and hair and painted

me with black and red oil colors and led me along barefoot-
ed and bareheaded on a very hot sunny day."

"That must have been very terrible for you, Mr. Sauer,"
said Colonel Smith.

"You have no idea. My neighbors, the people of this town,
turned their heads away as I was led through the street.
When a friend of mine saw me in that condition, he asked
the soldiers if he could give me his shoes and hat and made
the soldiers promise not to steal them. The officer gave his
word, but after six miles of hard marching, another soldier
came and took my shoes and gave me his old slabs, which
wounded my feet. Then I was taken into custody and had a
hearing before the provost. But good men spoke up for me,
and I was released. However, I was not allowed to return
until now."

"Well, Mr. Sauer, that is quite a story," Colonel Smith said.
"I wish I could show you some sympathy, but to be honest,
that is how we treat traitors here. You are an example to
others, a rather harsh example to be sure. Just remember, all
you had to do was swear an oath of allegiance to the American government."

"But we cannot swear oaths!" Christopher Sauer protested. "We Brethren take seriously what our Lord Jesus
Christ said when he told us that we should not swear by
heaven or earth or by anything, but to let our yes be yes and
our no be no."

"You know," Colonel Smith said, his voice was dripping
with sugar. "That's a nice thing you say, but what about
your son? Can you say the same for him? He is a British spy

and there's no denying that. And if we get our hands on him, there won't be any auction. We'll just string him up."

There was nothing to be said to that, Christopher Sauer knew. His sons were very active in the cause of Britain. And everyone knew that.

"Well, surely you will let me keep my clothes?" Sauer protested.

"Actually, according to my orders, we're to take your clothes," Colonel Smith replied, "except what you're wearing, of course, and anything valuable."

"Not my medicines, too? My father and I mixed those medicines. They are of no use to anyone else!"

"On the contrary. Medicines are quite valuable."

"How about my Bible?"

"Well," Colonel Smith smiled, "if I understand you correctly, your Bibles are especially valuable. We could get quite a lot of money from their sale, money that will go a long way toward establishing your loyalty when they go to supporting our glorious cause. Now please, sir, if you will just step to the side."

Colonel Smith went to the door and beckoned several soldiers to come in.

"Please escort Christopher Sauer outside these premises and keep him away."

But none of the soldiers moved. Not at first.

"You have your orders," Colonel Smith said, a little more impatiently.

"Sir?" one of the soldiers offered

"What?"

"Are you sure we should do this?"

"I'll have you on report," Colonel Thompson huffed. "This man is a traitor."

"But—," said the soldier timidly.

"Well," interrupted Colonel Smith. "Spit it out."

"The men are talking, sir, the other soldiers. According to what they say, the man who painted him and kept a part of his clothes took sick a few days later. A horrible pain, and nothing could stop it. 'Just like Herod,' he shouted. 'Just like Herod in the Book of Acts.' Then he said, 'Take them off, take them off!' meaning the clothes he had stolen, I mean confiscated, from Mr. Sauer. And after a few days of great misery, he died."

"I won't listen to superstition," Colonel Smith said.

"The men don't think it's superstition."

"Well, you let them know that if they are any kind of patriot they will do their duty, or be strung up like a traitor with no questions asked."

And that was the end of it. The officers sold everything. They sold the presses with the beautiful type. They sold the paper and the paper mill. They sold the leather for binding, and the thread and the gold for stamping, and the ink for printing, and the machines for making the ink. And Christopher's medicines. And his own personal Bible. Everything!

When it was over, Christopher Sauer stood alone—stunned. Where was God in all this? God had promised to be with him in the valley of the shadow of death! What about the promises?

But while he was standing there, a man timidly came up to him. He did not appear to be a rich man, or a poor man, but a tradesman. In his hands he was holding a parcel wrapped in old newspaper. There were other men behind him. Some Christopher Sauer recognized. Some he did not.

"Look at this, Mister Sauer. Look at what I have," the man said.

Christopher took the heavy parcel and pulled back just a bit of the newspaper. "It's a Bible—one of my father's Bibles."

"Yes, your father printed this and my father bought it when he first came here. My father was a laborer from Worms. He dug up peat. In Germany he could never afford a Bible of his own. But when he came here and tilled his own land and ate his own apples, he felt like he had come to paradise. But he couldn't afford a Bible, not at first. Your father told him to pay as he could, at no interest."

"Oh, yes. That sounds like my father," responded Christopher.

The man went on, "My father learned to read with these pages, and he would read aloud to my brothers and sisters and me. He always called it the Sauer Bible. Now look, the binding is worn from so much use. The pages are coming loose. Please, if I can provide the materials, will you restore this Bible? I know you are a proud man and will not accept charity, so I want to pay you. Will you bind it up again?"

Another man stepped forward at that moment. "And I have a building for you to work in. Perhaps together you can help me buy the right equipment so you can start binding books for others. Even if you have lost your printing press, there is much you can do."

"Please," said the first man, still timidly, as if afraid that the great Christopher Sauer would refuse him. "We have never forgotten your father. Or you. You have always put the community first. You and your father have seen to it that our children are taught and the newcomers fed and that the legislators do not forget us, even though we speak German."

First one and then another of the men came forward with offers of money and clothes and goods.

"We are your brethren," said one of them. "You took care of us. We will take care of you."

Then one more man came forward, holding a parcel very similar to the first man's.

"What is this?" Christopher Sauer asked. "Another Bible for me to bind? Soon I will have more work than I can handle," he laughed.

"No," the man replied. "Well, yes, it is a Bible. It's a Sauer Bible. But it doesn't need to be bound. It is for you. To have. I think a man named Christopher Sauer should own a Christopher Sauer Bible!"

Christopher Sauer II lived until 1784. Though he lost his press and all his goods, he worked hard as a bookbinder and paid back everyone who helped him get back on his feet. And because he no longer had to tend to several businesses, he had more time to travel and preach the gospel for the Brethren, visiting many churches in Pennsylvania to ordain ministers and deacons. His son Christopher Sauer III fled to London, where he managed to get a pension from the British government to make up for the losses his family had suffered. Eventually his family moved back to America.

The Sauer Press is now recognized as one of the most important industrial endeavors in the American colonies.

7
Mama Don't Allow No Piano Playin' 'Round Here

Henry Kurtz

1828, Poland, Ohio

There's an old song that goes like this:

> *Mama don't allow no piano*
> *playin' 'round here.*
> *Mama don't allow no piano*
> *playin' 'round here.*
> *I don't care what Mom don't*
> *allow.*
> *Gonna play this piano anyhow.*
> *Mama don't allow no piano*
> *playin' 'round here.*

It's a funny old song—and probably not true. Most parents love to hear music playing around their home. But the lyrics in this song are about all the different instruments that people like to play.

Mama don't allow no drum playin' 'round here.
Mama don't allow no drum playin' 'round here.
I don't care what Mom don't allow.
Gonna play this drum kit anyhow.
Mama don't allow no drum playin' 'round here.

A long time ago you could have sung this song about the Brethren. The Brethren loved music, but didn't allow musical instruments in their churches. Even though the Bible tells how God's people used musical instruments in their worship, some Brethren thought it was wrong to play the guitar, the piano, and the church organ. Maybe this would have been a good song:

Brethren don't allow no organ playin' 'round here.
Brethren don't allow no organ playin' 'round here.
I love the Brethren, but even so,
Gonna play this organ soft and low.
Brethren don't allow no organ playin' 'round here.

Henry Kurtz came from Germany to Pennsylvania in 1817 and became a school teacher. He was a man who loved education, loved to learn, loved books. Henry Kurtz also loved music and owned an organ made in his hometown in Germany in 1698.

Two years later he decided to become a minister and studied hard to do well at this new job. He was soon pastor of a Lutheran church in Pittsburgh, but when he tried to tell people they needed to live the way the Bible tells us, there was trouble, and he soon resigned and moved.

Henry Kurtz wanted to find a church where people tried to live like Jesus. In order to find other people who wanted to live like Jesus, and who might want to move to the same place to live together, he started a magazine. Henry thought that people should work together, take care of each other, read their Bibles, and worship as God's people.

But it was difficult to find enough people who wanted to live this way. Henry Kurtz and his family moved to Ohio in order to start the perfect church, made up of perfect people, serving a perfect God. But they never got the new church started.

Then Henry Kurtz discovered that there was already a group of people who were trying to live like Jesus. They lived near each other, worked together, took care of each other, read their Bibles, and worshiped as God's people. They were not perfect but they tried. These were the Brethren, and they were doing the things he had always thought the church should be doing.

In 1828 Henry Kurtz was baptized into the Brethren Church. If Henry Kurtz thought the Brethren were good enough for him, the Brethren also decided that Henry Kurtz was good enough for them as well. They asked him to become the minister of the Mill Creek congregation near Poland, Ohio, and that is where he stayed for the rest of his life.

Even though Henry Kurtz thought the Brethren did most things right, there were some things he thought needed changing. Henry Kurtz loved learning, and he thought the Brethren should be going to college. Henry Kurtz loved books and magazines, and he thought the Brethren should have a magazine of their own. Henry Kurtz also loved classical music, and he wanted Brethren churches to have pianos and organs.

There were other Brethren who loved the same things as Henry Kurtz. But some people weren't as patient as Henry. They believed that making a fuss was the only way. But Henry knew the Brethren were always changing. It was just that they had to be convinced that the changes agreed with the Bible. And sometimes that took a long time. Henry Kurtz loved the Brethren so much that he was willing to wait.

Henry Kurtz made his living as a farmer, but he also bought a printing press and began to print Brethren books. He printed hymnals and sermons and a New Testament in German.

Every year he attended Annual Meeting, no matter where it was held. The Brethren recognized that he was a good writer, and they made him the clerk of the Annual Meeting, so that he could keep a record of what was said and done there, to be shared with all the Brethren around the country. The Brethren were beginning to spread out from Pennsylvania into Ohio, Indiana, and Illinois. Some were heading out to Kansas. Others were heading into the South. It was getting more and more difficult for some Brethren to get to Annual Meeting, so they needed the reports from Henry Kurtz.

Because the Brethren were more spread out, it was becoming more difficult for the Brethren to know what was going on in all the churches. Henry decided it might be a good idea to start a magazine that would tell the news about the Brethren. He also believed that it was important to write things down so that people would not forget them. He talked about his idea with others. Some told him it was a great idea. Others said that it wasn't. They worried that printing a magazine might split Brethren further apart if they started to argue in its pages. Some worried that this might be a way of making a profit from the gospel of Jesus Christ. Others thought it would be too expensive.

In 1851 Henry Kurtz started his magazine to show the Brethren what it would be like. It would allow Brethren from across the country to write to each other and tell the news of what was happening in their churches. It would not only help them to keep track of each other, but it would also allow Brethren writers to write about the gospel.

Henry Kurtz did not worry about making a profit out of the gospel, because it was very expensive to publish a magazine, and it was not likely that he would make any money. He called the magazine *The Gospel Visitor*. In the first issue, Henry Kurtz told the Brethren that now they could teach each other and learn from each other. They could share the truth.

At first there were Brethren who still thought the magazine was a bad idea, but the more they read it, the more they liked it. After a few years, the Annual Meeting gave Henry Kurtz permission to continue to print his magazine. He had been very patient and the Brethren at last made that change.

Other people came to share the ideas of Henry Kurtz. One of them, named James Quinter, came along to help him. Together they began to print more materials. They worked together to help change the Brethren, but they were patient.

Some of those who were worried that having a magazine could cause trouble turned out to be right in one respect. There were other Brethren who started magazines that criticized the church or other Brethren. One of those was a man named Henry Holsinger. He had many good ideas. He wanted Brethren ministers to have more training. He wanted Brethren to be able to go to college. He wanted Brethren to have musical instruments in the churches. But he was *not* a patient man.

For a while Henry Holsinger worked with Henry Kurtz on *The Gospel Visitor,* but then he started his own magazine and over the years he criticized others very loudly. Even if he was right, he was not always kind. Eventually Henry Holsinger and some of the Brethren who wanted changes to come quickly left the Brethren and started their own church.

Over the years Henry Kurtz played many beautiful psalms and songs on the organ, but he played them very quietly and when he was alone. Henry Kurtz loved that organ. The man who built the organ had written these words on the instrument: "In the forenoon of September 23, 1698, I Johan Christoph Harttman, organ maker of Nürttingen, firmly closed this small wind chest. May God grant that many beautiful and spiritual psalms and songs be played and struck on this work to His name's honor."

When Henry played music on that organ, he felt like he was worshiping God, as the builder had hoped. He wanted the Brethren to change and to allow him to play the organ, but he continued to be patient.

Over time the Brethren changed in all the ways that Henry Kurtz had hoped for. The Brethren began to print books and go to college. They began to allow musical instruments in the churches.

Henry Kurtz was right about a lot of things, but he cared about the Brethren and didn't want to hurt people. He was patient, and gradually others came to share his ideas.

When you go to Annual Conference, you will hear Brethren sing. You will hear Brethren play the organ and the piano. You will hear Brethren play guitars and drums and harmonicas. You will hear Brethren play on the pipes. The Brethren love music and play all instruments!

Brethren like to hear that guitar pickin' 'round here.
Brethren like to hear that guitar pickin' 'round here.
All that music is allowed
So play that guitar nice and loud.
Brethren like to hear that guitar pickin' 'round here.

Henry Kurtz lived from 1796 to 1874. His magazine, The Gospel Visitor, *is still being printed today. Now it is called the* Messenger. *The organ that belonged to Henry Kurtz is more than three hundred years old. If you visit the Brethren Historical*

Library and Archives, you can see it and many Brethren books and papers that have been collected and saved for all generations of Brethren.

8

My Daddy Is the Best Preacher in the World

Samuel Garber

1858, Ogle County, Illinois

My name is Sarah
Garber. My daddy is
Samuel Garber and he
is the best preacher in
the world. I know this
because people really
pay attention when he
preaches. They care so
much that they throw
him in jail.

When I first heard that my daddy was thrown into jail for
preaching, I was very embarrassed and worried about what
others would think, but since then I have heard that a lot of

people have been thrown into jail for preaching God's word—like the Apostles Peter and Paul. But I thought these things only happened in Bible times, and not here at home.

We live in Illinois. I like it here. This is a free state. That means no one is allowed to own slaves. Daddy says that is one of the reasons we moved here. We used to live in Tennessee where there are creeks and hills and the people are very friendly. At least they used to be. But then these same people threw my daddy in jail for preaching the gospel and telling the truth.

Here's what happened. One day Daddy hitched up the horse and cart and told me that he was heading back to Tennessee. At first I wondered if we were all moving back, which would have been nice, because I missed my friend Sally. I had written her a letter once but I don't know if it even got there.

But Daddy said no, just he was going to Tennessee. He said he had business to take care of, and while he was there he might do some preaching. I told Daddy I would miss him and that if he saw Sally, he should tell her hello and let her know I sent a letter.

Then Daddy gave me a big hug and said he would come back as quick as he could. He doesn't like to be away from us too long, ever. I kissed him and we said goodbye.

I know Daddy worries about us and does not like to be away, but like I said, he is a very popular preacher and people want to hear him, and he said he must do God's work while there is time.

When Daddy got to Tennessee, a minister at a church that wasn't Brethren asked him if he would preach to them about

Isaiah 58:6. I have copied it out of our family Bible: "Is not this the fast that I have chosen? to loose the bands of wickedness, to undo the heavy burdens, and to let the oppressed go free, and that ye break every yoke?"

My daddy is a very smart man. You can give him any verse in the Bible and he will be able to talk about it. That is how our Brethren ministers preach. They don't know ahead of time that it is their turn to preach, so they don't know ahead of time what they are going to preach on, but they are always studying the Bible. Maybe they do not go to fancy schools like the ministers in some other churches, but if you are chosen by the Brethren to be a minister, it is because you know your Bible.

I am not surprised that people wanted to hear Daddy preach when he was in Tennessee. He was very well known and was always asked to preach. But now I wonder, did they pick my daddy because the other ministers there were afraid to preach? Were they *afraid* of their neighbors? Because this verse is about slavery.

Well, in Tennessee some people own slaves, and some people don't. And there are lots of hard feelings about slavery. In states like Illinois, people don't own slaves, but in the southern states they do. Daddy says that some people even say it is God's will that those people are slaves. We know that is wrong. God loves all people and does not mean for some of them to be owned by others. It seems like some people must read a different Bible than the one we have in our church.

Daddy says that it's not that easy. Sometimes people read the same Bible and think two different things. I guess so, but how can they believe in slavery? Would Jesus have owned slaves? I don't think so.

Yes, I think they must have asked Daddy to preach because everyone else was afraid. Sometimes I wish my Daddy was afraid to preach about the truth too, but he is not.

Daddy said he was very tired from the trip, but took care of our horse first and made sure he was all right before he went to the church, the Old Salem Presbyterian Church in Washington County. The man at the church welcomed him and called him Reverend Garber, which made my Daddy laugh. Daddy told him we don't call our ministers "Reverend." So the man asked, "Should we call you Father Garber?" Daddy laughed again because he has five kids. Daddy explained that he was a Brethren minister and that it would be enough to call him Brother Garber.

Daddy said the church was full of people who came out to hear him. They sang hymns, but Daddy said it was not like when our people sing. They also had a pipe organ. I wish I could have heard it, because we don't have one in our church—or a piano—because they are not allowed.

The man introduced my father and said he was there to preach on the great topics of the day. This made everyone sit up, because all anyone was talking about was slavery. Those people think slavery is right and that it comes from God. Now that is the devil talking—but they don't know that!

Now I know Daddy. He didn't want anyone to tell him what to preach on, because he wants to wait for what the Holy Spirit will tell him. He figured that everyone there already knew what they thought about slavery and that nothing anyone said in a sermon was going to change their minds. So he decided to preach about other things that matter. He told them all about Isaiah, how in Isaiah's day the rich were taking advantage of the poor and the powerful were hurting the weak people, but they still thought they were holy because they never missed church.

Then Daddy told them that it is the same now. He talked about how some people are caught up in sin. Some drink too much and love the things of this world too much, like food and fancy clothes and fancy churches. Daddy said you could see people squirm, because they wanted him to preach about other people's sins, but everything he said hit close to home.

He talked about justice and that Jesus will come back and what the judgment will be like. He talked about how God loves people and wants them to change. That's what Isaiah said way back then in Bible times, and that's what God is still saying. Daddy told them people carry around a yoke of sin on their necks, just like oxen in the field, and it is weighing them down, and all they have to do is throw off the yoke and let Jesus carry it for them and they will be safe.

Daddy said some of them were crying when he talked about what the world would be like if people took this verse to heart, how there would be no war and no talk of war, and how there would be love and peace and good will, union and fellowship, around the world. I heard him say that at our church many times, so I know what he would have sounded like.

Then Daddy told me that it must have been the Holy Spirit working, because it had not been in his mind to mention slavery at all. He wanted these people to think about their other sins, but he ended up talking about slavery anyway. Daddy said he didn't say much. He just said that slavery is one of the sins that Isaiah was talking about and that when he used to live in Tennessee he preached about this all the time. Daddy said that since he no longer lived in the state he would not say as much. But he said slavery was wrong, plain wrong, and that even if Isaiah were here he would also tell them so.

Well, the sheriff of the town and the officers who came with him jumped out of their seats. The sheriff was shaking so badly he couldn't talk for a second. Daddy said the sheriff's face was so red he thought the man would explode, so he said a silent prayer for him.

Some started shouting about lynching Daddy, and others called for tar and feathers. Putting tar on a person and then feathers could sometimes kill a person, but otherwise it would make the person very sick.

Then a minister of one of the fancy churches got up and said he would preach about this same verse from Isaiah later just to show that it had nothing to do with slavery, and he invited everyone to come and listen to him.

After singing a hymn, many people came to shake Daddy's hand and to tell him they agreed with him and that he was brave to say what he did. Some of them were ministers from fancy churches, who told Daddy that people had to hear what he said, but that they would not be allowed to say those things in their own churches. Daddy told them he was under the Lord's protection and that it was his duty to preach the whole gospel.

As Daddy was leaving the church, the sheriff and his men surrounded him. They were cursing and shouting threats, but Daddy just stood there and said nothing, which made them all the angrier. But nobody came to stand by Daddy's side and help him leave—not even those people who agreed with him or who said he was a very brave man. They all sneaked away.

When the sheriff told Daddy that he had to come to the court right away, Daddy said no. It was Sunday; he would come any day but Sunday. So they said he should come on Thursday.

In the meantime Daddy preached everywhere, again and again from the same verse. Every church was packed because everyone wanted to hear his sermon. Although people were afraid to speak up, many of them believed that slavery was wrong.

The more Daddy preached, the angrier the sheriff and others became. In the newspapers they said Daddy should be killed with no trial—just killed.

When Daddy showed up at the court on Thursday as he was told, the sheriff's hands were shaking so much he couldn't sign the arrest papers and somebody had to sign them for him. Then they talked in the court about whether to have a trial. There were some people who told lies about Daddy. They said all he preached about was slavery and that he was a bad man and no one trusted him, and that's why he had to leave Tennessee a long time ago.

Meanwhile, there were those who were planning to catch Daddy and kill him when the court was over. So they sent a slave on a mule with the news to those who were going to help with the killing. But something scared the mule and he stumbled and threw off the poor slave, who broke his neck and died. So the message to kill Daddy never got to the bad people. Later, when news of the accident was put in the newspaper, nobody said anything about how sad it was that the slave had died. It only mentioned that the slave was worth a thousand dollars and that the man who owned the slave had lost lots of money. This is how terrible some of those people were!

The judge listened while the people lied about Daddy. Then he listened to Daddy, who said he was not afraid, because he knew the Lord was with him. Daddy answered all the questions and told the truth, because that is what Brethren do, no matter what.

Finally, the judge said there would be a trial in September, many months away. Even though Daddy was planning to come home before that, he said he was willing to wait for the trial.

Then the judge told him that he would have to wait in jail unless he paid five hundred dollars for his bail. That's more than a year's wages for lots of folks! Daddy didn't have that much money with him. He said he would have to arrange for some farm animals to be sold and that he would be glad to wait until the money was sent. That's when other Brethren who lived in the area said they would pay Daddy's bail.

It turned out that Daddy came home before the trial! The other Brethren told Daddy that things were getting very bad for them because of Daddy's preaching. They said that folks were starting to threaten them too and saying they were all bad people. They told Daddy that the court did not really want to have the trial, because it would just make people angrier and that Daddy should just go back to Illinois. If

Daddy left before the trial, they would lose their five hundred dollars and Daddy didn't want that to happen. But Daddy didn't want other people to be killed, so he said he would leave. If the Apostle Paul could be lowered in a basket from a window in order to escape bad people, then he could certainly ride a horse out of town to save the others from danger.

When Daddy got home, he was able to send the Brethren some money. And at Annual Meeting the people were asked to give money to help pay Daddy's bail so the folks would not lose all their money, but they only got thirty-one dollars.

Now people are talking about a war because of this slavery. They talk like it will be just horses and flags and singing and drums and people charging, and all of it happening very quickly. But many of the Old Brethren talk about what they heard from their grandfathers and grandmothers about how bad the wars were in Germany before they came to America. They said that it's not just soldiers who die, but also the families left behind, little children and babies and mamas and daddies and grandpas and grandmas. They say that war lasts forever, that farms are lost and homes are burned, and it's like the angel of death passing over the houses. Who will be spared?

But folks are saying there is no way to stop slavery unless there is a war. What will happen? Will there be a war? Will slavery end? We all pray in church for the will of God and the end of these great troubles, but how it will come out I do not know.

What I do know is that my daddy is the best preacher in the world.

❦

Years later Sarah wrote about her memories of her father. Many Brethren suffered during the Civil War because they did not believe in slavery. Books like The Olive Branch, *first published in 1907 by the Brethren Publishing House, help people remember the suffering that can come when peacemakers stand up for what is right.*

9
A Train Full of Trouble

P. R. Wrightsman and the Civil War

1863

He was known as P. R. Wrightsman, but his first name was Peter, and he came from Limestone, Tennessee. As the train rattled and thumped on its way to Richmond, the capital of the Confederacy, he looked out the window at the lush and green Virginia countryside. Facing the open window, he breathed in the smell of growing things, something that all Brethren farmers loved. If he closed his eyes, it smelled like paradise, but when he opened his eyes he saw something in the fields that took away his joy.

Everywhere in the fields of cotton and tobacco and corn, he could see the black slaves working their lives away, their backs bent over in the hot sun, arms moving, or scythe swinging, sweating and maybe close to dying.

Peter was a Brethren minister and a doctor and a farmer. He loved the chance to heal people, to make them well with God's help. He was young for a Brethren minister, the youngest one any knew of. He was often happy, even proud, to be such a young Brethren minister, but now he wished it were not so, because he had been asked to travel to Richmond on a very dangerous mission.

"Why me?" he had asked when the other ministers told him he had been picked for the mission. "Why did you pick me when I was away? You knew I was away at school, learning how to be a doctor. I am the youngest minister. You should pick someone with more experience."

But they had insisted. He was the one who was best, they said.

Many Brethren had been arrested and thrown into prison and now he was going to Richmond to seek their release. The Brethren had told the authorities that their Christian beliefs did not allow them to fight in the army, and the Confederate Congress had passed a law saying that Brethren did not have to go to war if they paid $500. That was a fortune, but many Brethren paid the money. Yet, after paying the money, many were arrested anyway for not going to war. And Peter was worried that he might be thrown into prison as well. He might even be killed.

But that was hard to think about, so he looked out the window again and was sorry he had done so, for there were the slaves. And here and there, riding on their horses, were the slave owners.

Peter did not think of these slave owners as devils. They were his neighbors and some were his friends. They were the people he had grown up with. But they were wrong and they were sinning and he knew God was grieved at what they were doing. He also knew that most people in the South were poor, hardworking farmers, who did not own slaves.

As he rode along, he reflected on the war going on, a war between the South and the North in America. Everywhere there was war fever. The newspapers told stories of the battles that sounded so exciting, but every time Peter saw a list of the dead, he thought about how each one of those people must have suffered in pain and agony before dying, and how each person's family grieved and wondered if it was worth it. He thought about all those soldiers, his neighbors and friends even, who were marching this way and that over the countryside for a cause they thought was right. He heard they were dying from sickness as often as from a gun wound. They did not have enough to eat, which also meant they were stealing from the people they were supposed to be fighting for.

At first he had thought of all these people as evil, but when the Confederate soldiers came to steal from his farm, surprisingly he changed his mind.

It was in the spring, when, without warning, the Confederate soldiers came over the hill on a raid. They had shouted and threatened as they stole his eleven horses, his crops, and even the rifle that he used to catch food for the family.

There were no slaves on his farm, of course. Peter and his family did all the work themselves. As the soldiers looted, Peter stood in their midst, saying nothing and wondering if they were going to kill him. He remembered how afraid he'd felt. They looked so evil to him then, as if they were devils. Each time they stole something he thought, What will we do? He was especially frightened when the last horse was stolen. There was nothing left for the Confederates to take. He was afraid, but he stepped into the barn and prayed, "Dear Father, save me from these men. Have mercy upon them, turn them from their evil course, and save thy servant."

As he prayed, he felt God's presence. Stepping out of the barn, he immediately saw the soldiers in a different way. He saw how hollow their faces were from hunger, how frightened they looked, as if they were the ones who were in danger. He saw that their clothing was ragged, and some did not have shoes.

Peter felt God's pain for these men who were straying so far from God's plan. And he felt God's love for these people, even though they were doing wrong.

One of the soldiers had even come up to him, seeming almost as if he were sorry, and told him he was so hungry.

Quickly Peter replied, "Yes, we are commanded by our Lord Jesus to feed the hungry. Let me get you something." And he went into his house and brought out bread and butter for all of them. When they asked how he could be so kind to them after what they had done, Peter told them that Jesus said to turn the other cheek and that Brethren tried to do what Jesus said to do.

He could tell as they rode away that they had much to think about. Perhaps his actions would prevent them from harming others. He did not know.

Suddenly there was a shudder of the railroad car, and he remembered where he was. The car was filled with the smoke and conversation of many Confederate soldiers. Some of them were playing cards, some drinking whiskey. Peter saw that some were looking at him in a strange way when they thought he didn't notice. He knew it was because he looked different. As a Brethren minister, he wore simple dark clothes and a broad-brimmed hat. He wore his beard long, without a mustache, after the style of the Brethren.

Then he saw that the one man who was not dressed as a soldier wanted to talk to him.

"You, sir," the man said, "I notice that you are very quiet. I am a minister. Tell me about what you do."

"I am a minister also, of the Brethren faith."

Some of the soldiers put their cards down to listen.

"You are a minister, too?" the man said. "Where did you study for the ministry?"

"We don't send our ministers to a special school," Peter replied. "We pick them from among those who know the Bible best and are respected by everyone. I went to school, but to be a doctor, not a minister."

"Isn't that unusual?" the man asked.

Peter explained that it wasn't unusual, that all Brethren ministers worked, some as farmers, some as doctors or smiths or grocers or storekeepers.

When the other minister asked him what the Brethren believe in, Peter paused. He knew that his answer wouldn't be popular, but if God chose for him to share these beliefs, it was important to do so. "Many of the things we believe in are the same as all churches. We believe that Jesus changes our lives, that we must be converted to this new way of life. We also believe in baptism by dunking people three times into the river."

"Is that why some people call you Dunkers?" the other minister asked.

Peter smiled. "That is where it comes from. Also, we do not conform to the world. We are different. Our communion includes the washing of feet because that is what Jesus did. Our communion includes the meal we call the Lord's Supper. We do not swear oaths—we do not take each other to court."

He swallowed and then said, "And we do not go to war."

As soon as he said that, it grew very quiet in the railroad car, except for the rattling of the wheels and the sound of the engine in the distance.

"Don't you think we all ought to fight for our glorious Confederacy?" the minister asked.

"But the Bible says 'Thou shalt not kill,' " Peter responded.

"But this war is an exception," insisted the minister.

"Christ made no exceptions. He told us to love our enemies. So we cannot go to war with them." Peter felt as if every eye was on him. He wanted to answer these questions in such a way as to make the other people happy so they would leave him alone. But he had to answer with the truth.

Then the other minister asked him if he didn't believe George Washington was a good man.

"I never saw him," Peter said, not really wanting to answer. He knew everyone thought George Washington was very special, the wisest man who ever lived.

"Well, don't you believe that God used George Washington to fight the Revolutionary War and to set up the government?" asked the other minister.

Peter answered, "God has often made use of one individual or nation to carry out his plans concerning another." Then it was almost as if someone else told him what to say. He added, "And you believe that God set up this government by Washington, do you?"

"Yes. Everyone does."

"Then what do you think God will do with you for trying to tear down what he set up?" Peter heard himself saying.

For a moment Peter asked himself why he had said that. He could see it made the minister angry. It made everyone in the railroad car angry. Instead of saying something, the other minister glared at him with an angry expression, got up, and stomped out of the railroad car.

Some of the soldiers began to curse at him. They called him names and told him what they thought ought to happen to him. Some threatened him.

But from the moment he opened his mouth, Peter discovered he felt very peaceful. He had said what was important to say, and now he was in God's hands. For the rest of the trip no one spoke with him, and when he walked off the train in Richmond, no one followed him.

After arriving in Richmond, the walk through the city made him feel uncomfortable. So many people, so many horses leading so many carts, the feeling that great events were going on. There were boys selling papers giving the war news. The people walked around as if there was a great deal of importance in everything they did.

But underneath what seemed like a high level of excitement, Peter thought he also detected a spirit of gloom. This was the capital of the Confederacy, and people seemed to know there would be more death and destruction before this terrible war was settled. Some people stopped at the street corners to look at the lists of the dead and wounded that were posted everywhere. Occasionally someone would recognize a name. Then there would be a look of shock and sorrow and sometimes silent weeping. Peter said a prayer for them.

When he appeared before the Confederate legislature the next day, Peter felt like a very small person indeed. He could see there were many suspicious faces when he explained that he was there to seek the release of Brethren prisoners. But there was some sympathy as well. One congressman in particular asked about the Brethren and why Peter believed as he did.

"It is very simple, really," Peter said. "The Bible tells us we shall not kill, and we always believe and obey the Bible. Yet we are also called to serve other people. You know that your soldiers have gathered our crops and fed their troops, and we have not resisted. But ask yourself, every time you have taken away one of our Brethren boys and made him march and drill, what sort of soldier has he been? A very poor sort."

There were some nods of agreement at that.

"You can make us fire our guns, but it turns out that when we are firing in the direction of a man, we are very poor shots. Is this not so?"

This time there was some laughter.

"On the other hand, we are very good farmers and good citizens. We were born in the South. This is our home, our native land. Yet some of our Brethren have fled to the North both before the war and during the war. When one of us leaves, who will till the soil? Not your soldiers. They are already busy enough."

"But why," said one congressman who seemed a little angry, "should we not call you traitors if you are not willing to fight for our new country?"

"All countries, even good ones, are only temporary," Peter replied. "When we first came to this land, we were grateful to the British for the religious freedom they offered. When the colonists rebelled and formed a new country, we were good citizens of the new country. And so we remain. It is our wish to bind up the wounded and feed the hungry and worship God as we see fit. That is all we ask."

In the end Peter convinced them to release the prisoners, for they had already paid their bounty. Soon Peter found himself on another train, heading for the prison camp. There he found his fellow Brethren in poor shape, for they had been badly treated in prison. It wasn't easy to secure their release, for one officer stopped Peter and pushed a gun against his throat and threatened to kill him.

But Peter said a silent prayer for him and just waited. Another officer scolded the attacker and told him to step back. "Don't you wish you had a brother who cared for you so much he would risk his life to come and get you?" he asked. And Peter walked out with the prisoners.

It was a happier train ride home. Instead of a trainful of Confederate soldiers who might be suspicious of him, now Peter was sitting with his Brethren friends, and they sang many Brethren songs all the way back home to Tennessee.

***

At first the Brethren were able to live in peace again, but as time passed, the war began to go badly for the southern states, and resentment grew. But P. R. Wrightsman persisted in showing his faith and Christian love to even the most dangerous soldiers, at one point inviting them to love feast when he found them surrounding his church.

Peter took charge and very carefully explained to the Confederate soldiers how Jesus washed the feet of his disciples to show that the greatest among them needed to be the greatest servant, willing to do anything. He compared the meal to the Passover, when God had led the people out of slavery to freedom, and how they wished to be led from the slavery of sin to freedom in Jesus. Peter also spoke of the bread and wine and how Jesus shared these after eating the Passover meal with his disciples, and how they were to think of him every time they ate the bread and drank the cup.

After it was over, Peter shook the hands of all the Confederate soldiers and thanked them for coming. Some of them told Peter he must come to their churches after the war and tell these great things to their friends and family. Peter promised he would try, but he also knew that many of these men would die in battle in the weeks ahead. He was glad that they had been able to share in the meal of Jesus together.

When the war was over, Dr. P. R. Wrightsman was appointed to a committee that helped make sure that Brethren families in the South received aid as they sought to recover from the devastation of war. Later, he moved to Kansas, where he helped to found the first Brethren insurance agency, which is now known as the Mutual Aid Association.

10
My Mama's Not Afraid of Nobody

Ann Rowland

1863, Longmeadow, Maryland

My name is Billy Rowland. I want
to tell you that everyone is afraid
nowadays. The War Between the
States keeps on going and no one
knows when it will end. Maybe it
will never end. The soldiers from
the North march south and the
soldiers from the South march
north. And more and more people
are being killed.

I go to the German Baptist
Brethren Church. We are Brethren. We do not go to war and
believe all war is wrong. But that does not keep us safe from
danger. Because people know we will not resist, it often
makes things more dangerous for us. People take things
from us because they know we will not harm them.

Some say Maryland is a northern state, but others say we are really one of the southern states. Although we have slavery here in Maryland, most people don't have slaves. And we don't want to leave the Union, although some people think we ought to.

Because we are in the middle, there have been some terrible battles in our state. Last year there was a battle in the cornfield at Sharpsburg, not far from here, and more than twenty-three thousand were wounded or died in just one day. That's more people than in most towns. All gone. The Confederates used the Brethren church there for their headquarters, and it was all shot up. They also stole the Bible, but that is nothing. What is terrible is that so many people died.

People never know what is going to happen. There are always rumors, stories saying General McClelland from the North is coming through, or General Stonewall Jackson from the South. Everyone is worried that the soldiers will steal from them. People are hiding. People are afraid.

Except my mama. My mama's not afraid of nobody. Her name is Ann Rowland, and everyone knows about her. And they know if my mama wants to get something done, then it will be done. And no matter how frightened other people are, my mama is not scared.

It's always been that way. Mama doesn't talk about this stuff, but I learned it from the folks in our church, who told us because they know she doesn't brag.

One of the things they told us was that in the old days only people with property could vote. Ordinary folks who worked could not vote. Now that didn't matter to our family, because when Pap married Mama, he got Mama's farm, because she was an only child and her parents left her four hundred acres. So Pap could vote.

When President Jackson talked about giving the vote to common folks, it was Mama who went about the county telling people why they should support him. If she heard that someone was against giving ordinary people the vote, she would go straight to that person and let him know how she felt. It was very hard for folks to stand up against her.

Some Brethren say we should not get involved in politics, but Mama said the world would go sour if we put our heads in the sand. She said you have to take your head out of the sand and take a look around. After that they did what she said.

Mama also spoke out against the evils of alcohol and how people who sell it are hurting families. They used to give out beer to all the harvesters during the harvest, and Mama said that was hurting the harvest, not helping it. And even those who didn't agree with her had a hard time arguing with her when she went after them.

Then there was the time when a new school was built, and some of the folks at the church said that we should buy the old school and make it into a new meetinghouse for church. My older brothers and sisters were going to that school, and they said it was falling apart and the rain would come in through the roof. But folks said it was good enough for a church even if it wasn't good enough for a school—that we could just fix it up a little and not spend so much money. My mama visited folks, and she and Pap got them to come and vote against buying the school. Then she and Pap donat-ed some of their own land for the new church. Mama wasn't ever afraid of work. She and Pap and we kids laid the foundation. We even burned the bricks, and Mama and Pap paid for the new church all by themselves. So it was not just a fixed-up, broken-down church, but a good building. It is still there.

After that Pap hurt his back when he was lifting big stones for our new barn. He was sick for a long time before he died. It was hard for all of us, and very sad, but Mama said we still had to get in the crops and run the farm. There were enough of us to do the work. Some of the kids were all grown up then, and I was very little, but we all worked hard. We kept the farm going and never went hungry. Not ever.

But that was all before the war, as I said. At first everyone said the war would be fast. In Maryland we are in the middle of the country—south of north and north of south. Those who liked the North said the North would lick the Rebels, and those who liked the South said they'd be the winners, and everyone talked like it would be grand entertainment. Everyone wanted to buy the newspapers and they would talk about it in town. When one side would win a battle, those folks would whoop and holler, and when the other side would win a battle, they'd crow about it.

But the war just went on and on. After the big battle near Sharpsburg, when we all heard the shooting and men were put up in makeshift hospitals in homes and churches with their legs or arms cut off and bleeding, some dying and the rest just hollering and moaning—well—after that nobody thought the war was a game.

Then we just began to worry. There was talk that the Confederates were going to invade the North. Some of the folks said they'd never win the war that way, because England would take the part of the South and then President

Lincoln would have no choice but to stop the war. Folks were very tired of the war. By now everyone was.

All this meant the Confederates would come through Maryland. And that meant the great General Lee would be leading them.

Everyone knows about General Lee. They say if it weren't for him the South would have lost a long time ago. They say he is smarter than the other generals and always wins.

Then one day the word came that the rumors were true. General Lee was coming. All of us got to work, hiding all the food we could. We knew they would take something. If they didn't find some food, they would burn everything. But we wanted to hide something for ourselves. We had a secret spot above the smokehouse where we hid the meat. Nobody knew about it, not even the deacons at the church. We made sure it was packed with food and moved the stones so it looked like nothing was there.

And then there were the horses. Folks said there was no way we could hide the horses. We knew the armies always stole the horses. But we had one horse, Old Jen, that was special, and we needed the one horse. So we got the storage room ready. It was like a cave, built into the rocks right next to the barn, and if you put some beams and boards nearby, it looked like nothing was there. We made sure there was plenty of good hay so she would be fine.

Well, General Lee came, and all the army. They took our church, the one Mama built with Pap. The General himself and all his staff took it over for their headquarters. No one knew what to do. If he said he wanted it, then he could have it.

We have a beautiful Bible that we read from when we have church, and folks thought that it would be taken along with all of the communion things and anything else that wasn't nailed down. That's what they did at Sharpsburg, you know. They took the Bible and never brought it back. When one of the deacons came to Mama and told her what had happened at Sharpsburg, she knew immediately that she didn't want that to happen at our church. She came to me and said, "Billy, come with me."

We left the farm and went right to the church. That's when I saw the soldiers. The officers were dressed fine, in fancy gray coats with gold buttons. They wore hats, and some of them had swords that hung at their belts. They walked with a swagger as if they were important.

The soldiers were different. They looked pretty ragged, and lots of them didn't have shoes. They looked mean, but they also looked tired. They looked at Mama and hollered at her to get out of the way, to go back home, but she didn't even look at them. She went right to the church and said she was going to talk to General Lee.

Now there were guards there, who held out their guns and told us to stand back. I was afraid and started to back up, but Mama gave me a look, so I stayed with her and we walked right past the guards. They looked like they weren't sure what to do. But that's how Mama is—when she wants something, she gets it.

All the benches were moved around. Normally there are benches on one side for the men and on the other side for the women, but this wasn't for church. Because there are no backs on the benches, a bunch of them were pushed to the wall so the folks could sit on them and lean against the wall.

Some of the officers sat up and took notice when we came in, and a couple of them started to laugh. General Lee was sitting by himself on a straight-back chair at a desk he brought, and he was writing. When he saw us, he stood up.

Then all the officers stood up. One of them said, "What is the meaning of this? You get out of here right now!" But General Lee put up a hand to quiet the officer.

I thought General Lee looked very old and tired. But he was very polite to Mama and asked her what her name was and what he could do for her.

Mama got right to the point. She said there was nothing he could do for her, but she had come to get the Bible of the church, because she did not want it stolen. This made some of the officers look angry, and I wondered if we would get into trouble, but there was Mama, looking General Lee right in the eye, like she does to anybody, and telling him what she was going to do. And when Mama tells somebody what she is going to do, then that is what she is going to do. Like I said, my mama's not afraid of nobody.

Well, that's when General Lee told Mama that he would like to use the Bible for morning devotions, like when we have family devotions at home. He said it would be his word of honor that he would take care of it, and that they would leave the church just the way that it was, and nothing would be taken.

Mama thought about it for a second, and I wondered if she was going to take the Bible anyway, but later Mama told me the only reason she didn't because she hoped it would do General Lee some good, what with him being a traitor and fighting for slavery and all. Mama always said God wants to save everyone, and it's never too late for a sinner. So she said that would be good enough for her.

So that part came out okay. The church is still standing and our Bible is still there.

But we still had to deal with the soldiers. They were stripping the bark off trees to bake their bread on, and that is bad for the trees. So Mama baked bread instead and gave it to them. Some folks said that was helping the enemy, but Mama said that nobody is our enemy and that Jesus would want us to give bread to anyone who was hungry.

But meat is different, Mama says. Mama also cooked meat, but she sold it to them. They bought so much that when it was all gone, Mama decided to cook some more and told me to watch the fire while she went to cut some meat. She took a big knife and headed back to the hiding place. Well, some of the soldiers started to follow her to see where the hiding place was, so they could come back later and steal the rest of the meat. Mama looked them square in the eye and held the knife out and said, "Don't you dare take another step."

That's all she had to say. They just stood there and waited, and when she came back she cooked up the meat like nothing had happened, and they paid their money like they were supposed to.

Later Mama explained that the Bible says we are to be wise as serpents and gentle as doves, and that she never said she was going to hurt anybody. She told those fellers they were not to take another step and they didn't. And if they had taken another step, she said she just wasn't going to cook up any more meat. And if they'd harmed her or me, then she would have gone to General Lee and left them to him.

Finally, the time came when the soldiers took the horses, like we knew they would. They even found Old Jen and took her, too. We had put Old Jen in the hiding place, like we planned, but when the soldiers took the other horses, they made all kinds of noise, because they did not want to go. And that made Old Jen lonely. So she began to whinny and neigh, and the soldiers heard her. The next thing you know, they followed the noise and figured out where she was.

"Well, how are we going to run a farm without a horse?" Mama said. And off we went—right up to the church, and this time the guards didn't even try to stop her. General Lee was still sitting there behind the desk, like he had never left, and when Mama came in, he stood up and greeted her by name: "Mrs. Rowland," he said, "what can I do for you this time? You can see the Bible is still here."

So she told him about Old Jen and about running the farm on her own with her children, and her husband being dead and all. One of the officers said a Bible was one thing, but the army needed horses. But General Lee—he had to answer to Mama, and so he told her that if she was brave enough to come ask for her horse, it would be given back to her.

They found the horse double quick, because when General Lee spoke it was almost as important as if Mama says something. And this time General Lee sent a guard to our house for the rest of the time he was there, which wasn't very long.

The soldiers went on to Pennsylvania to a place called Gettysburg, because they heard there were shoes there, and they needed shoes. There was a great battle for three days. And that was the start of the end of the war, but not before many more were killed or wounded.

Later on, Old Jen was stolen anyway, and it was hard on the farm. More important than keeping the Bible is that I learned from Mama that we should never be afraid to tell folks to do what is right. Even if they are powerful or important like General Lee, we have to tell them what is right. She said God comes first. We follow Jesus and that's good enough for us. Mama is gone now, but that's something I always remember.

The story of Ann Rowland's bravery in the face of General Lee was something her children and grandchildren always remembered. Other people remembered too, so when a history of the Brethren in Maryland was written, she had a very important place in that book.

11
Too Late to Say We're Sorry

John Bowman

1866, Annual Meeting

The folks who walked by the open
field near the Antietam Meetinghouse in Pennsylvania had to stop
and wonder for a moment if the
circus was coming to town. There
were great wooden posts and
stakes and long ropes and canvas
as long as fields. Strong men were
straining as they swung sledge
hammers into large stakes thrust
into the earth. Others groaned as

they dug post holes or pulled on thick ropes. The great
swaths of canvas were stretched until the large tents and the
smaller pavilions were lifted into place. All was being made
ready for a wonderful meeting.

But this was not the circus. These tents were for the Annual Meeting of the Brethren. This was a special Annual Meeting, because the Civil War was over. For many in America, it was a time of great anguish and resentment, as well as many fears, because both the winners and losers eyed each other with suspicion. A nation torn in two was struggling to become one again.

For the Brethren this was a time of joy. They had remained one church throughout this war. While other religious groups had split in two over their loyalties for and against slavery, the Brethren had proclaimed that Jesus was their only ruler and their only allegiance.

Nevertheless, it had been very dangerous for most Brethren to travel and visit each other. Brethren in the North had heard from afar of the persecution and trials that some of their sisters and brothers in the South faced. At the time there was little they could do for each other. Only a few brave souls, like John Kline, had dared to cross the Mason-Dixon Line, and he had been murdered for his bravery.

Now the Brethren could finally come together in love to worship God, to help each other, and to settle those questions that always come up when the Brethren get together. Not only was it going to be a time for worship and singing, but also for a great deal of talking and eating. It was good to be together.

Seeing the Brethren hard at work dispelled any thought that these tents were for the circus. Men with long beards and broad black hats had removed their coats and were straining to put everything in place. Wagons of supplies were unloaded—large pots and stacks of plates and cups, spoons, knives, and forks.

Soon a kitchen was in full operation in a separate tent. Fires were being set, and a willing army of cooks gathered their supplies. Women in dark dresses, gray and black, with black bonnets, were hugging and kissing each other, then settling into their tasks. There was a clatter of knives on wood and whisks in metal bowls. They tore the tops off of carrots and hurriedly peeled potatoes.

There were beef roasts and hams and great stacks of eggs, sacks of flour and noodles, cakes, crackers, and kegs of butter carried in by two or three staggering men. Most of all, there was laughter. Four or five years had passed since many of these women and men had seen each other, and there was so much to say to one another.

Children ran in and out of the tents. Some were shooed away when they tried to help themselves to a treat, but most were allowed to leave with an apple or a cookie. Some stayed, insisting on helping in whatever way possible—running errands, fetching water, and carrying items here and there.

More Brethren arrived. Some were bringing pies—apple and berry and mince. Others had jars of pickles, with cobwebs still hanging from some of them that had been stored in the root cellars of the Brethren.

Only a few days before, the railroad workers had finished their mighty labors. A special spur had been built, a track that split from the main line to bring a large number of expected passengers from across the nation to this one place. Now the trains were steaming up, and people were streaming out, walking the short distance to the field that was no longer empty. Annual Meeting was underway.

"Stop running in the kitchen, Ezra!" Miriam Booz scolded her son, but he was already gone when she added, "I have told you that three times!"

"You don't sound too angry," Agatha Royer chuckled.

"It's just kids playing. How often do they get together, really? They're so excited!" Miriam said.

"And how long since we've been together. Five years! Can you believe it? Five years! You look so good. I heard you were starving in the South during the war."

Miriam looked serious for a moment. "We were starving toward the end. The soldiers from both sides had stolen all the supplies they could find. What little food we managed to hide we fed to the children in the dark of night. The little ones learned never to ask for food while it was daylight so no one would know we still had some. And there would have been more food for the children, but Papa would often take food to the other children."

"Brethren children?"

"All children," Miriam said. "Of course, their parents often threatened him or called him names because he didn't fight in the army, but he would still go out after dark and leave food on the doorstep of this neighbor or that neighbor, when he heard there was need. He would knock on the door and then flee so they would not see him."

"But if they had seen him," Agatha said, as she peeled another potato, "maybe they would have thought better of him."

"Or maybe they would have found out we still had food and come to take the rest," Miriam answered.

The sound of singing was coming from the great tent, where a growing throng of brothers and sisters was coming together.

"Miriam, if you would like to join them, there are plenty of us here to take care of things."

"No, I can hear fine, and I can sing fine from here. Maybe later. Now it is just good to be with you and the other sisters and brothers. Ezra!" she added, "are you back? Why aren't you with the other children?"

"I just wanted something to eat!" he answered.

"No," said Miriam. "You will spoil your appetite."

But Agatha was already handing him a shiny red apple. "Now run along. Go play!"

"Thank you!" he shouted as he ran off.

"You will spoil him," Miriam scolded with a smile. "You're still the same. That hasn't changed."

"You know what has changed? The children don't play war anymore. Remember before all of this? We had to scold them for making guns out of sticks and pretending to shoot each other. They learned it in school with the English children, or playing with their neighbors. But they all know what war is like now. I hope they remember."

"They'll remember. It's the next generation of children we will have to teach."

"Sisters, how are you?" said a young man as he walked into the tent. "Do you have anything for a hungry traveler?" At least his face was young, but his beard was already showing a little gray. Everyone who had survived the war looked older than their years.

"Yes, I do, Brother Wrightsman," Miriam said. "Don't you remember me? You preached at Knob Creek many times!"

"Sister Miriam!" he said. "I'm sorry. It's light outside the tent and it looks dark in here."

"You're excused. Sister Agatha, this is Brother P. R. Wrightsman, the doctor. What will you be doing here at Annual Meeting?"

"I've come to ask for help for our brothers and sisters in Tennessee and Virginia and throughout the South. I am sure Annual Meeting will organize the raising of money for those who are suffering, who lost everything. But also I am here for this wonderful cooking."

"For that you get a piece of mince pie," said Agatha, cutting out a slice for him. "Would a pickle do as well? There's no hot food yet, but soon! But, before you leave, Brother Wrightsman, would you help us put some of this beef into the broth? I think the water is getting hot."

For a minute the minister helped the women load large pieces of meat into the pot.

"Now before you go," Miriam said, "tell us what else will happen here at the meeting."

"There is some talk about reorganizing the Annual Meeting to make the business go better. And there is a query about dress and what the sisters and brothers are wearing. And then there will be—," he paused, "the business about Brother Bowman. Brother John A. Bowman of Tennessee."

"Oh," said Miriam, sadly. "It's a little late for that isn't it, now that he's dead?"

"Who was Brother Bowman?" piped a small voice at their feet.

"Ezra, I thought I told you to go play," his mother said, but Brother Wrightsman had knelt down to talk to him.

"He was a great preacher, a great man, Ezra. He was known far and wide as one of the most trusted elders. He would preach about temperance to those inside and outside the Brethren. And he stood up against slavery even though he lived in the South and it wasn't safe to do that. He was a very important brother. But during the war some men came to steal his favorite horse. They were wearing the gray of the Confederacy. The horse was terrified. When Brother Bowman tried to comfort his horse, one of the men shot him dead."

"So like John Kline he was murdered?" Ezra asked.

"Yes, John Kline was a great man, and a martyr," Wrightsman said. "And Brother Bowman was also a martyr."

"But I don't remember people talking about John Bowman in church."

P. R. Wrightsman looked up at Ezra's mother, as if asking permission to talk. Miriam Booz nodded, giving permission.

"Well, that is because he was disfellowshiped, Ezra."

"What is disfellowship, Mama?" Ezra asked.

"That is when the Brethren decide you are not in accord with the order," she replied. "It means you are not a member of the church anymore."

"Like when Auntie Ada wore the hat when she visited her friends in the city?"

"Yes, like that. When she was disfellowshiped, she was not allowed to worship with us or to take communion. Some would not even say hello to her when they passed her on the street. She had to admit she was wrong and then promise not to do it anymore."

"Well, what did Brother Bowman do wrong?" Ezra asked, turning to Brother Wrightsman.

"He took another brother to court. We Brethren do not take each other to court. It says so in the Bible. We have to settle our disputes among ourselves."

"But why did he?"

"It wasn't for himself. It was Brother Bowman's duty to settle the estate of one of the members who died. The money was needed for the family the man left behind. That brother would not pay the debt to the estate, because he said the man to whom he owed the money was dead. So Brother Bowman took him to court and made him pay. And for that he was disfellowshiped."

"That doesn't seem fair."

"Well," Agatha said, "I think that's why they're going to talk about it here."

Ezra didn't seem to be satisfied. "But why do we have to disfellowship people, Mama? Just because we don't agree?"

"It's how we have always done things," Miriam said.

"But what if I am bad, Mama. Will you disfellowship me?"

"No, of course not. Have a cookie. I will always be your mama."

Ezra thought for a moment. "But what if I get a hat from a friend at school and want to wear the hat? Would you disfellowship me from the family, Mama?"

"Why ever would you take such a hat?"

"I wouldn't, Mama. But what if I did? Would I stop being your son?"

"No, never," his mother insisted. "You will always be my son. I will always love you. You know that God always loves us, even when we sin. And God always searches for us like the lost sheep until he finds us. Why would I treat you any differently?"

"Well, then, did we stop loving Brother Bowman?

"No, no. You are asking hard questions. Have another cookie will you? Say, isn't that your friend Willy? Ask him if he'd like a cookie, too."

The three adults watched Ezra run off, waving the cookie and hollering at his friend.

"So what will happen if we say he should not have been disfellowshiped?" Agatha asked.

"Well, as you know, after Brother Bowman was disfellowshiped, he continued to preach and teach, to marry, to hold love feasts, and to baptize. A good number of people still thought of him as their minister. If Annual Meeting says he should not have been disfellowshiped, their baptisms will count," P. R. Wrightsman said. "And those people will be able to say they are Brethren without having to be rebaptized."

Miriam shook her head and began to chop some carrots for the stew.

"You know, this is all very sad. It's too late to say we are sorry when someone is dead. There has to be a better way for us to handle things when we do not agree."

"I am sure there is," Brother Wrightsman said. "I hope we find a way soon. I don't think there will be a lot of disagreement at this Annual Meeting because we're so happy to see each other again. But there has been a lot of talk about changes, a lot of changes. About dress and communion and education for ministers and Sunday schools."

"I've heard that," Agatha said. "You know, we Brethren do make changes, but we have to be patient with each other sometimes and really listen."

"I hope we will," Dr. Wrightsman agreed. "We've done it in the past. Remember when the western Brethren and the eastern Brethren got back together finally? But if we don't learn from the past, we might not be able to preserve our unity."

"How could that be?" Miriam wondered. "During the Civil War the whole country fell apart and we stayed together. Now the country is at peace. Do you think we would really fight each other and split up?"

"I hope not," Agatha said. "But I really wonder what will happen."

After the war the church helped to raise money for those who suffered for their faith. But the church also struggled to face issues of change. Years later, Annual Meeting disfellowshiped some Brethren who could not agree with each other. The church split three different ways, with more splits happening later on. Today members still disagree, but they no longer exclude each other from membership.

12
Believe It or Not

Phebe E. Gibbons

September 25, 1871
Lancaster County, Pennsylvania

Phebe Gibbons looked out
the window as the train rattled through the Pennsyl-
vania countryside. She was
a reporter who liked to tell
her readers about many
strange and delightful
things they had never heard
of. Her next assignment was

the Brethren love feast. She wondered if people would believe
what she would have to tell them.

As the train rumbled into Lancaster County, Phebe knew
the people would be different. Many of those she saw were
called Plain People. While the rest of the world wore bright
colors and followed the latest fashions, while everyone else
argued about changes, the Plain People stood out because
they changed so slowly. They wore simple clothing, dark col-

ors, and to folks from outside, they probably all looked the same. During the Civil War some people thought of the Plain People as traitors because they would not fight, but now there were more people who thought the war had been a great mistake and that the ills it sought to correct would take a long time to heal.

Phebe knew more than most about the Plain People. She could see the differences between the Mennonites and the Amish. And she knew about the Brethren, who many people called the Dunkers, because of their method of baptism.

Phebe wanted to tell her readers about the Brethren and about their communion service called the love feast. It surprised her when she first wrote to Elder Long at the Cornwall Church of the Brethren that he encouraged her to come and observe. She thought that perhaps the service would be closed to outsiders. She had even thought she might have to put on a disguise and try to sneak into the love feast. But no, Elder Long wrote to her and said that visitors were always welcome to observe and that there would be plenty to eat and drink and watch. He also told her to bring no money, because she would be their guest.

When the train stopped at Mount Joy, Phebe found a hotel room, thinking she might need to come back to the hotel to sleep. After that, she hired a horse and buggy and a driver, who took her five miles to the village of Cornwall. It cost two dollars, a pretty considerable sum.

"There it is," the driver said, pointing to the new Brethren meetinghouse. Phebe leaned forward to get a look at the neat frame building, brown with white window frames. But there were no doors facing out to the highway. Phebe learned that they faced toward the woods instead.

Brethren were gathering outside with many teams of horses. They had straw and bedding and a good deal of food in their wagons. She asked one of the women if the love feast had started.

"No," came the reply, with a slight German accent. "It won't start until one o'clock tomorrow."

"Oh my," Phebe answered, disappointed. "I guess I've come out for nothing." Then she explained, "My name is Phebe Gibbons. I've come to write about the love feast. But I don't want to get in the way."

"Nonsense," laughed the woman. "There's plenty to see and do today. My name is Margarite Burkett. Please come with me."

They passed through a meeting room inside. Margarite led her up the steps to the garret, where the straw was being laid down. "This is where many of us will sleep tonight. I'll show you the women's side."

"You will sleep here?"

"Well, yes. That way we can talk and visit and laugh all the night long. It's great fun to see so many of our sisters again. You'll stay with us here tonight, won't you?"

"But I'm not Brethren," Phebe explained. Even though she had tried to avoid any extravagance in her clothing and had worn no jewelry, she still felt very, well, bright and gaudy, especially as she looked around the room filled with busy women.

"That's okay. We Brethren believe we are all brothers and sisters. You are our guest."

"Well, thank you," she answered, not yet certain if she wanted to stay. Then she asked, "What makes the women's side different from the men's side?"

Margarite laughed. "We have a little room to the side over here. You can look in. It is for the ones with babies."

There were a couple of chairs and bedsteads and a candle for those who might need to take care of their babies.

"We'll get a better look tonight," Margarite said. "Now come, I'll show you the basement."

As they descended the stairs, Phebe asked, "Won't we keep the men awake if the women spend the night talking?"

Margarite smiled. "Oh, they make more noise than we do."

The basement smelled like heaven, if heaven smells like fresh bread and strong coffee. There were large loaves of bread, pies in baskets, and coffeepots everywhere. It was divided into a kitchen, a cellar, and a dining room, and there was a hard dirt floor beneath their feet. Phebe watched as a man and a woman put all the food in order.

Although most were speaking German when she arrived, they spoke English in her presence—to be polite, she supposed. Phebe did not want to tell them she understood a little German herself, not yet anyway.

"How did you find out about the love feast?" asked one very tall, thin man. His beard was thick and gray.

"I read about it in our paper."

"No Brethren would have put it in a paper. But never mind. I am glad you are here," he said.

Phebe stayed for awhile, but decided she would not spend the night, because she had left her change of clothing at the hotel. She promised she would stay the following night.

However, Margarite would not let her leave without giving her bread and butter and a cup of coffee.

"Now even though we say the meeting will not begin until one o'clock," she warned, "don't believe it. We all get up early because we're so excited, so get here early for the singing. And you, John Brower, you are doing nothing."

"I am *not* doing nothing," protested the chubby fellow who fanned himself with his hat, as though he felt too warm. His face was red and he was blowing on his own cup of coffee.

"You and your wife can take Miss Gibbons back to her hotel—she is not planning to stay the night here. That will save her the fare."

Phebe protested, but John Brower would have none of it, and soon the buggy was hitched and she found herself back at her hotel, where she spent some time writing up her notes.

Phebe slept well enough, but she woke to a steady rain. Once again she hired a local buggy to get her to the meeting-house, where she was met at the door by a stocky man, bearded like all the men. He smiled at her and said, "Are you Miss Gibbons? I am Elder Long, and I was hoping to meet you today. I wondered if you had any questions. Please come to the basement with me where we'll have a meal."

Phebe Gibbons carefully observed that the long tables were covered with a strip of white muslin. She would tell her readers that the men sat on one side and the women on the other, that everyone got bowls with spoons, into which was poured very hot coffee containing milk but no sugar.

Oh, how her readers would delight, she thought, when she wrote to them about the fine Lancaster County bread, and the thick slabs of butter, and the apple butter, and the pickles, and the pies.

"Who provides this food?" she asked Elder Long, who sat near her. "Is it all done by the local congregation?"

"Yes, much of it. We meet ahead of time and decide who will bring bread, or butter, or pickles, or meat, or pies. Some of them give money instead. But we all contribute. You see, many people from other Brethren congregations for miles around will come, and it is our joy to share this with them. And then we will go to their love feasts, too. All spring and all fall we are going to love feasts, as many as we have time for. It is like the Bible says in Isaiah, Why do you pay for food when you can have all you want? It's all free. Most of us are farmers and we have plenty. Everything we have is for everybody."

"And what about the food that is leftover?"

"We give it to the poor," Elder Long explained, "no matter what church they attend."

"May I ask another question? Why is it the men are serving at the tables?"

"Well," a woman seated nearby said, "It says in the Bible we are to serve each other. And so the women cook and the men wait on the tables."

"Why is that?"

"Well, you wouldn't want the men to cook," she replied and all nearby laughed.

"Where does it say this in the Bible?" Phebe asked.

"I'm not sure," the woman said.

Elder Long thought for a moment and said, "I suppose the text 'Bear one another's burdens' would suit."

When they went up to the meeting room, Phebe watched as all the men and women greeted each other like old friends.

An older woman then took her by the arm. "Please sit by me. Here is a hymnbook. It is in English and German. Maybe I can answer your questions. My name is Eleanor Murphy."

Phebe was surprised. "But isn't that an Irish name? Don't they sometimes call you the German Baptist Brethren? I thought all of you Brethren were German."

"That's not so. Our families take in orphans and raise them, and we naturally remain Brethren. There are one hundred thousand of us Brethren, and though many are German, there are plenty of us who aren't. There are even former slaves who are Brethren. Of course, some people say we should change our name so people will know that not everyone in the church is German."

"When will that happen?"

Eleanor shrugged. "If that is to be, it will come in time. Many times we will talk over something for years, even decades, at Annual Meeting, and when we are in unity then we make a change."

Phebe watched as the men kissed the men and the women kissed the women. This she knew, from having seen it before. If the Brethren were known for anything, it was for sharing the holy kiss, which was mentioned several times by the Apostle Paul. Since it was in the Bible, Phebe knew, the Brethren said they must do it. Other Christians told her those verses were not really meant to be obeyed, but with the Brethren, if the Bible said to do something, they did it.

Phebe took her place on a wooden bench. It was much harder than she was used to, and after a time she felt a little uncomfortable, but she noticed that everyone else seemed to bear it pretty well. The women sat on one side, the men on the other, and the children were sprinkled among all of them. At the front of the meetinghouse there was a single bench on which all the ministers sat. Instead of preaching from a pulpit raised high above the congregation, as Phebe was used to, they sat at the same level as the rest of the people.

The service that followed was very long, with much preaching and singing. The meetinghouse was full, and she was surprised by the large number of babies. No matter if they cried or gurgled or squirmed, no matter what noise they made, it did not seem to bother these people when they preached or prayed.

"To us," Eleanor whispered to her, "it is like the wailing and sighing of the wind. It is normal and natural for the infants to be among us."

There were many sermons, all but one in German. Though she could understand much of what was said, at times Phebe found her attention drawn to the windows. Outside she could see a lot of young people, some dressed in gray or black like the Brethren, some in bright colors. The girls stood together talking, and the boys stood in another group, both groups seeming to make a point of not looking at each other.

On and on the meeting went, but as sunset approached, some of the Brethren rose and pulled up small tables that lifted up from the backs of the benches.

"We will go downstairs while they finish preparations for the love feast," Eleanor Murphy said, taking her by the arm. Again Phebe descended the stairs, where she found that the women were cutting very large loaves into four pieces to get them ready for the love feast. She was invited into the kitchen, where she was given more bread and butter and coffee.

"Okay, I think they are ready," Eleanor told her. And they went back upstairs to the meeting room.

Phebe watched, trying to remember everything. The men sat at one set of tables, and the women at another. Hanging lamps shone down on the tables where great platters of meat were set on top of tubs of broth. But instead of eating, one of the ministers read from the New Testament; then four men took off their coats and wrapped towels around their waists. Two of them washed feet and two of them dried. Those four took their seats and four others performed the same action. Phebe saw that the same thing was taking place among the women.

It was very quiet there inside the meetinghouse, but many in the village had gathered outside and were either watching through the window, or simply talking as if nothing special were going on.

Apparently others were as curious as she was. All this, she was told, was done in imitation of Jesus. Everything that would happen that night, they told her, was found in the Bible. And Phebe wondered for a time if she had not wandered into some chapter of the Bible that was still being written. Was this what the early church looked like in the days after Jesus lived and died and rose again? Still, she couldn't but feel that the Bible was being acted out before her. Was this what the gospel meant when it said the Word was given flesh to dwell among us?

But Phebe herself was hungry and her mind turned back to the food. She wondered if the food would get cold while they washed feet, but when the plates were lifted off the bowls, steam rose, filling the room with a heavenly smell. Only those who were baptized could take part and eat together. But one of the sisters told her there was plenty of food for everyone. One of the young girls, not yet baptized, invited Phebe to come along with her, and the two of them joined others to eat in the basement. Phebe found out there was rice and barley in the broth and that the meat was very good.

When she went back upstairs, the service was still going on. Now bread and wine were placed on the table and covered with a white cloth. Again the ministers read from the Bible, this time about the Last Supper. All joined in a hymn that Phebe recognized, "Alas! And did my Savior bleed?" She sang along as well.

The communion bread, she noticed, was more like a cookie or hard cake. One of the ministers said, "The bread that we break is the communion of the body of Christ." The brothers and sisters broke off a piece of bread in turn. Then the wine was passed around. When they were through, they quietly rose and left the meetinghouse.

And that was the end of the quiet. A short time later, Phebe was up in the attic with the other women to spend the night. For a good long time, they all talked about the day's events and any news there was to share. Many of them asked Phebe questions about herself and her writings and her travel.

Phebe slept on a grainbag filled with straw, with a good blanket. It was more comfortable than she supposed. For a long time she lay awake. In the dim light of a candle, Phebe looked up at the roof. It was clean and clear of cobwebs. She was surprised that everything was kept so nice for the love feast. They had not missed a detail. Still unable to sleep, she rose and sat in a chair by a small window. All around her was the noise of gentle breathing. This was very normal to all those who were there, but she was still trying to make sense of things.

It was getting late, or rather very early, for at length she saw Orion the Hunter rise, and after him Sirius the dog star. It would not be long before daybreak. What should she tell her readers, she wondered. And would they believe her? Finally she gave up. Phebe lay down and went to sleep.

Morning came quickly. Phebe heard the noise of people running outside the church. The children were playing.

"We'll be having breakfast soon," Eleanor Murphy told her. "More of that meat, I think, and whatever pies and bread are left."

"And coffee?" Phebe asked.

"Of course," Eleanor smiled. "Always the coffee."

Phebe went back to the chair by the window, sat down, and looked out. Two young girls were making a baby laugh. An old, fat minister was standing near them, smiling, and some of the men and women were standing in little groups, talking away. Despite the fact they must have been talking together all weekend, there still seemed to be so much to say.

Then Phebe understood. It must be called the love feast because these people loved each other. They weren't any better or any worse than other folks she had met, but they seemed to be one family, no matter what their background. They weren't all German, after all, and they weren't all from this part of the country. But wherever they came from, however they got here, whatever their background, they were brothers and sisters. They were Brethren. This was a family built on love.

Phebe knew she would write about a bed made of hay and about all the talking and about the food, of course, and yes, about the coffee; and certainly she would write about the love feast itself, the feetwashing and the meal and the bread with the cup. But most of all, she would have to make her readers understand that these people loved Jesus and loved each other, and to them that was the most important thing in the world. It wasn't their clothes or how they acted at church that made them different. It was the love.

In 1963 a publisher in Lebanon, Pennsylvania, reprinted Phebe Gibbons' articles so that more people could read about the Plain People in Pennsylvania Dutchland. Even though Phebe Gibbons was not Brethren, her article about the Dunker love feast is considered an important source to help us remember how people used to do things in the mid-nineteenth century.

13
Who Gets the Credit?

John Lewis

August 23, 1877, Elmira, New York

"Help! Help!" Mark Twain, the famous writer, was standing by the side of the road when he heard the two women screaming. It had been a hot day, with heavy humidity, the kind of day that made him glad he was far from civilized parts.

Here at Quarry Farm, his sister-in-law's estate outside Elmira, New York, he didn't have to wear his white suit with shirt and tie. Most of all, he liked working in the little ivy-covered house she had built for him so he could write without being disturbed.

The sun was beginning to set. Many of the folks who had been visiting were starting to head home. Ida Langdon, a relative of Mark Twain's, and her little daughter and the child's nurse, Nora, were among them.

As he came out of the writing house to take in the cooler, late afternoon air, Mark Twain spotted the two women and little girl in Ida's cart, drawn by a young gray horse. But he did not pay much attention at first. He had just published a very popular book for children called *The Adventures of Tom Sawyer*—a book about the carefree days of his childhood on the Mississippi River.

Now everyone was expecting Mark Twain to write another great book about children. He was trying to write about Tom Sawyer's friend Huckleberry Finn, but it was hard to keep on writing. The story was missing something, some character who would tie everything together. Mark Twain hoped that by stepping outside he might think of more ideas for his book. But now he was alarmed. He could hear someone hollering.

"Help! Help!"

Looking out beneath his bushy eyebrows, Mark Twain felt his heart jump into his throat.

Something had spooked the horse and it was running out of control. The women and little girl were sitting in the buckboard of their wagon, which was careening wildly down the road. Sometimes only two of the four wheels seemed to touch the ground as everything rocked back and forth, up and down.

Twain knew that the road leading away from Quarry House was very steep and had many twists and turns. The wagon was sure to hit a rock or a rut and spill over. And a horse moving that fast could never turn in time.

Mark Twain's wife ran up to him. "Ida's horse is running away!" she shouted, as if she expected him to do something.

Mark Twain found himself running toward the wagon, which was already heading away from him, but he knew he couldn't catch up. He'd seen it before. The horse would only stop when the wagon tipped over, tossing the animal through the air. The women would be thrown as well, perhaps under the horse or the wagon, or along the side of the road. They would be badly hurt, perhaps even killed, with their necks broken in the fall.

If only there were someone who could stop the horses! But he knew that if an ordinary person found himself facing a wild horse dragging a cart, he would probably save himself and jump out of the way.

The writer huffed and puffed. There was no way he could get there in time, nothing to do but try to help the women— if they survived. There was dust in the air and dust in his lungs. He was coughing badly, but still he ran on.

Mark Twain wanted to shut his eyes. He did not want to see the two women and the little girl dead on the side of the road, but he knew he had to run until he was absolutely sure there was nothing to do. There was a turn ahead in the road, and beyond that he knew he would be looking down. Then he stopped in his tracks. He saw something amazing.

***

John Lewis had his hands on the reins as he drove his cart up the hill, but his mind was not on the road. It was on his troubles.

John had lots of troubles, even though he had never gone looking for them. John was a hard-working man, but he was also black, and in nineteenth-century America, that meant trouble. He had never been a slave. He was born free and stayed free all his life. Nevertheless, a lot of opportunities that other people had were closed to him. Nothing ever came easy. Things cost more when he tried to buy them, if people would sell to him at all.

John Lewis had a load of manure on his wagon. He was climbing the steep road to Quarry Hill to pick up his wife who worked there as a servant. They would then return to their own farm, where a lot of work still waited for him. John was used to working hard, but no matter how hard he worked, he had to borrow more and more money. He was deeply in debt, and there didn't seem to be any way out.

What really made John Lewis sad was that he couldn't worship with his church any more. Long before the Civil War, he had joined a group called the Brethren. Though they were all white people, they had welcomed him to their church, the Meadow Branch congregation near Westminster, Maryland. Over time he had belonged to different Brethren congregations, depending on where he found work. Then during the Civil War he had moved north, because even free Blacks were in danger of being made slaves in the South.

Although Quarry House was full of nice people, it reminded him of all the things he didn't have. The folks were kind to him and loaned him money so he could keep his farm, but their life was not his life.

The one good thing about traveling up to Quarry House was getting the chance to talk to Mark Twain, who was a very good friend of his. Twain was always interested in what John Lewis was doing and did not treat him like a black man or a white man. He just treated him like a person. To John Lewis, it was almost the same as when he was with the Brethren.

As these thoughts ran through his head, John Lewis suddenly heard a terrible noise. Up ahead, careening down the road out of control, was a cart with two women and a little girl. He could see the terror in their faces. He could see the horse, full of panic, eyes wide, with foam coming out of its mouth. The buggy was heading straight for him.

John Lewis could have saved himself by jumping out of the way, but he never hesitated. He could see there was a turn in the road ahead where he was certain the cart would roll over, killing everyone. There was a fence along the road ahead of the turn. He slapped the reins and drove his horse and cart ahead until his cart made an open-ended V with the fence. The out-of-control horse would have to run between the fence and his cart.

He could see the wild horse, all the muscles sharp and taut, the dust kicked up on the road, with the women screaming. John had no idea who these people were, but that didn't matter. He jumped from his own cart and waited until the runaway cart was close. He waited until the horse was upon him, nearly running him down. Then, leaping at exactly the right moment, he grabbed the horse's reins and pulled himself up into the cart.

With the strength he had gained working hard all his life, John pulled back the reins and roared and hollered at the horse. To his amazement, the cart came to a sudden stop.

The women were still screaming, almost as if they could not believe they were now safe. Then they began to cry in relief and hug John Lewis. Once he was sure that everyone was okay, he turned the cart around and began to drive it back up the hill, taking the women and little girl back to Quarry House where they could recover, safe and sound.

***

Mark Twain stood at the top of the hill in shock and disbelief. He had expected to see the cart on its side, its wheels still spinning, with Ida and her daughter and Nora pinned beneath, dead or horribly mangled. Instead, the two women and little girl were smiling and sitting next to none other than John Lewis. Ida was waving. She looked very pale and shaken, still a little frightened, but she was smiling and said bravely, "Well, we're still alive, aren't we?"

The whole family gathered around the cart and around John Lewis. Everyone was slapping his back and shaking his hand, but the modest man gave the credit to someone else.

Mark Twain had always liked his hard-working friend, but he was amazed at the sacrifice this man had made to help others without thinking about what it might mean for him. He had risked his life without hesitating. This meant that John Lewis was a different kind of man than others whom Mark Twain knew.

"If God saw fit to use me as the instrument for saving these women, then let us give God the credit," Lewis said.

"Oh," Ida said. "Folks can say there is no God, but I know the Lord put you there to stop that horse."

John Lewis laughed. "Then tell me, if God put me there to stop the horse, who sent the horse there in the first place?"

Later, Mark Twain took John Lewis aside and asked him more about the Brethren.

"John," he said, "that is some beard that you wear. I have only seen that sort of beard on certain Mennonites and other free thinkers."

"The Dunkers wear it too," John replied, "the people that some call the Brethren."

"What attracted you to the Brethren?" Twain asked him.

"There are many churches," John Lewis said, "but their chief goal seems to be popularity. There is no difference between the members and the world. They don't seem to pay much attention to the Bible. Now the Brethren, they teach the whole Bible. They want people to live out the Bible all their days, and not just on Sunday." He went on to tell Mark Twain about baptism in the river and about feetwashing and the love feast. He explained how the Brethren stood against war and how the Brethren had always stood against slavery and had accepted him as one of their own.

"But now you are living so far away from the Brethren," Mark Twain said. "How can you say you are one of them still?"

John Lewis explained, "I read the Brethren magazines like *The Gospel Visitor* and the *Christian Family Companion*. By doing that I can find out what is happening in the churches all over the country. I can read the sermons of my brothers in Christ, too."

Mark Twain was impressed. He, too, was against war and was not impressed with some of the other churches whose members seemed to live two lives. They were holy in public but took advantage of others when they thought no one was looking.

Suddenly Mark Twain had an idea for his new novel. In his book all the people who seemed respectable were pretending to want to take care of Huckleberry Finn, but each person wanted something from Huck. They were all trying to change Huck. They didn't love him the way he was.

Mark Twain decided he would take one character, though, a slave called Jim, and show that here was a person who cared about Huck just the way he was. He would have Jim risk his life for Huck and put Huck first. The bravery and love that John Lewis had shown in saving the lives of the women was the sort of bravery and love that Jim would have. But Jim's love and bravery would change Huck. Even though Huckleberry Finn had been taught that black people were not as good as white people, Huck would change and try to help Jim escape.

Now that he had a new idea, Mark Twain was excited about writing his book again.

The next day the people at Quarry House made up an excuse to get John to come over to the estate. He arrived to discover that the family was throwing a surprise party in his honor. They gave him presents, and Mark Twain gave him a collection of all the books he had written. The family cancelled all the money he owed them, and they gave him a great deal of money besides. Though he had asked for nothing in reward, the family was grateful for his bravery and quick action.

John Lewis used the money to finish paying for his farm. He continued to work hard and remained a friend of Mark Twain all his life. And he continued to keep in touch with the Brethren by reading his Brethren magazines.

Many years later he was able to help a Brethren church in Maryland. The church stood on the ground where the Civil War battle at Antietam had taken place. It was the bloodiest day of the war. More than twenty-three thousand people were wounded or died in one day. In that battle a soldier named Nathan F. Dykeman stole the Bible from the church. The man later settled in Elmira, New York. When he died forty years after the battle, survivors wanted to return the Bible to the church. But no one knew if the church was still there.

However, someone knew that John Lewis was Brethren, and they asked him if the Brethren church was still there in Antietam. Because John Lewis read his Brethren magazines, he knew where the Bible should be sent. Today that Bible is on display at the museum near the Antietam Battlefield. The Brethren church is still standing at that place as well.

Mark Twain's novel Huckleberry Finn *has been called the greatest American novel. Some hated the book because it showed a white boy and a black man learning to get along as close friends. But Mark Twain believed that all racism was wrong, and he wanted*

people to know that a man like Jim could display the same bravery and love as Twain's good friend John Lewis.

John Lewis died in 1906 and is buried in Elmira Cemetery not far from Mark Twain's gravesite. In 2000, the Brethren Historical Committee raised funds and placed a simple marker on his grave.

14
Love or Money?

David Emmert

1877, Juniata College, Huntingdon, Pennsylvania
Sometimes you have to make choices. David Emmert could make a million bucks, or he could touch a million lives. Can you guess which choice he made?

David was born in 1854, the eighth of nine children. His family lived near the Antietam Battlefield not far from Hagerstown, Maryland. He remembered very well the sounds of the canons and rifles and seeing the soldiers marching back and forth on the day of that now famous Civil War battle. David's father was one of the ministers of the congregation that met in the meetinghouse seen in widely published photos taken after the Battle of Antietam.

Brethren didn't go to war, but they were called to serve others, so the Emmert home became a hospital for both

Union and Confederate soldiers. The family also fed all who came to the house.

One of the casualties of the war were the children who were left without families, children whose parents were either killed or took sick and died because of the conditions left by war. And life's circumstances also made orphans. Sometimes women died in childbirth. Sometimes fathers or mothers would take sick and die. In many situations, other family members would take in the children if they could, but times were very hard, and many of these children went to orphanages, which in those days could be very dangerous places.

From a very early age, David tried to help orphans who lived near him. He tried to teach them to read and to draw pictures. He did what little he could, but he knew that when he became an adult he would find other ways to help children who had no families.

When David was only three years old, he discovered that he loved to draw. David realized that art was a way of honoring God by creating in a small way what God does in a big way. To David everything was beautiful—broken plaster, the shadows cast by the firelight, blotches of mud that suggested bigger pictures. Everything had a story.

David first used a pencil or crayons to create art, but he soon began to mix his own paints, using household items. His brother Jonathan, who was ten years older, encouraged David to draw and to paint.

But Jonathan soon went off to school and became one of the first Brethren to graduate from college. Many of the Brethren weren't sure they approved of colleges or even high schools. Some of the Brethren thought too much schooling was bad for their children. If they could read the Bible and handle money, that ought to be enough. David's father was one of those Brethren who thought college was a bad idea and even said to Jonathan, "I would rather see you dead than get an education." It was just a coincidence that Jonathan died only a few years later, but it left David feeling very sad. He decided that he wanted do something to carry on his brother's work.

That meant teaching, but David had not gone to college, because he did not want to disappoint his father. In 1872, when David was eighteen, he moved to Waynesboro, Pennsylvania, to work at a company that made farm tools. There he met a man named Jacob Zuck, who immediately recognized that David was a genius.

David was able to capture the beauty of trees, making them every bit as individual as people. He could capture the ripple of running water in a drawing. His pictures of buildings proved to be longer lasting than the buildings themselves!

In 1876 Jacob Zuck was one of several Brethren who founded the first Brethren college, Juniata College in Huntingdon, Pennsylvania. And in 1877 he insisted that David Emmert become the art teacher.

David not only taught art, but he also created art for the college catalog and made sketches of many of the buildings in the town of Huntingdon to raise money for the school.

One day in 1877 David created something that should have made him very, very famous. He stopped to see a man named J. C. Blair, who ran a stationery store in Huntingdon and one day hoped to sell his stationery products across the country. David was in the store to buy a notebook for a class he wanted to take at the college. J. C. Blair sold composition books, which had lined paper, but David wanted something else—a notebook without lines. So he decided to make it himself right there in the shop.

David took a piece of newsprint and cut it into sheets that were 5¾ inches by 8½ inches. He stacked the sheets together and nailed some carpet tacks through the paper into a piece of pressed board. He had invented the tablet and didn't even know it.

That tablet still exists today with David's notes on it. He found he could use the tablet for writing or for sketching ideas that would lead to finished pictures. J. C. Blair soon discovered that many people wanted tablets just like David's. It wasn't long before Blair decided to add a paper cover, and he asked David to design it.

The tablet was so popular that it was soon sold everywhere, and J. C. Blair's business grew and grew. The cover drawing included a pencil, so J. C. Blair had to sell pencils as well as other stationery items. Ironically, it was J. C. Blair who became famous for the tablet, not David Emmert.

But David wasn't interested in being famous. Nor was he interested in money. J. C. Blair offered to share the profits from the tablets, but David said no. He had other things on his mind.

About this time others were noticing that David was a great artist. On more than one occasion, David would attend a special school for artists, where famous artists would admire his work and encourage him to devote his life to art. But David was always drawn back to the school. Nor could he forget his childhood dream of helping orphaned children. The thought of helping children was far more important to him than anything else.

Juniata College was founded at a time when the economy was going through a depression. At the time there were orphans everywhere, and David enlisted the help of the college students to assist him in feeding the orphans and giving them clothes. David Emmert realized that he loved the children even more than he loved teaching art.

In those days things were very different for orphans. Sometimes the orphaned children were kept in the same buildings with people who could be dangerous, such as the mentally ill or even criminals. The children who grew up in these places were often treated very badly.

Sometimes adoptions could be even worse. At that time there was such a thing as "orphan trains," whereby orphans would be sent by train to a distant church. Farmers would show up at the church, pick the children they wanted, and then expect them to work very hard for them, often under harsh conditions. David Emmert noticed that many of these children were growing up to be criminals themselves.

He wanted to change things. He wanted every child to have not only a family, but a good family. So he founded two homes for orphans and helped start a third. And he also hired people whom today we would call caseworkers, who got to know the kids and the people who wanted to adopt them and made sure that there was a good match.

David Emmert published magazines to help promote these homes, and he filled the magazines with illustrations that he drew himself. These drawings were so attractive that people would read the magazines just because of the pictures. This helped him raise money for these causes.

David struggled to devote time to teaching and art as well. Sometimes he spent more time at the college, teaching art to other people. Sometimes he would have time to work on his painting and illustrating. But he always turned his attention back to helping the children. He worked so hard that he often took sick, sometimes very sick. But he kept working for others. Some of his best art went for free to his magazines and to the college to help the orphans and to help Juniata. And when he returned to teaching he would work very hard to teach as many as seven classes at once. But this schedule did not prevent him from being active in church, where he was a deacon in the local Brethren congregation. Those Brethren who were against education thought that once someone left home for college, they would leave the church, but David Emmert remained active in the church his whole life, even while he pursued his love of knowledge. There were too many things to do, and never enough time to do them.

Money was never important to David. Even though he founded the homes for orphans and helped run them, he always made sure that his salary was very small, no more than he would have earned as a teacher.

Though David Emmert could have been a very rich man, he chose to touch millions of lives instead. There were those he taught, who grew to love art and to bring happiness through their work. There were his own paintings and drawings, which brought joy to the people who owned them. There were his homes for children, and through these he brought happiness to the children and to the families who adopted them.

And there were those millions of tablets created, as it turned out, for others whom he would never meet, people who filled the pages with their own drawings, bringing God's world to life and delighting others.

As both an artist and a teacher, as both a father to three sons and one who helped orphans, David Emmert was always busy trying to do more in the name of God.

Before David Emmert died in 1911 at the age of 56, he realized that there were some things he would never complete, including many paintings. David told his friends that he hoped he would be able to paint pictures in heaven.

What do you think? David Emmert could have made a million dollars, but he chose to touch a million lives. He could have been famous around the world. Instead, he brought joy to orphans, to his students, to everyone who knew him. Did he make the right choice? What would you have done? What will you do with your life?

David Emmert was one of the first Brethren artists and one of the first teachers at the first Brethren college.

In 1976, one hundred years after David created that first tablet, the United States celebrated its bicentennial. As part of the celebra-

tion, the Smithsonian Institution thought that David Emmert's original tablet was such an important invention that they asked to borrow it to have on display. But Emmert's biographer would not loan it.

If you ever think about going to a Brethren college and get a chance to tour Juniata College, make sure you ask to see some of David Emmert's artwork.

15
Who Will Harvest the Corn?

Anna Kline

Linville Creek, Virginia, 1883

"Grandfather, what is wrong with Tante Anna?" Elizabeth asked.

Michael Kline, his fork in his hand, paused for a moment. It was odd, he thought, that Elizabeth would bring him the very first piece of pie she had baked before even taking a taste herself. It was a berry pie, made from some of those put up last summer, some of the berries as big as his thumb.

"You've asked that before, Elizabeth, and I've always told you that there is nothing wrong with Aunt Anna," he said at last.

"I'm not a child anymore," Elizabeth replied. "I'm old enough to do just about everything on this farm. Last year you and Grandmother moved into the small house with Tante Anna, while our family moved into the big house."

"Well, that is normal. When one family gets older—and smaller—and all the children have grown up, it's time for the grandparents to move so a growing family has a little more room."

Elizabeth persisted, not allowing her grandfather to change the subject: "This morning Tante Anna was singing the song again—the one Uncle John wrote—the one we sing sometimes at church." There was a lot Elizabeth wanted to know. So she sang the song.

> *We'll sure go home as soon as freed,*
> *A holy life with God to lead!*
> *Go home, go home and that indeed*
> *As soon as God the way will speed.*

"That was the song she sang this morning, over and over."

Michael Kline closed his eyes and thought of the first time he'd heard that song. It was when his uncle, the Elder John Kline, was released from the jailhouse. John and the other Brethren men had refused to join the Confederate Army, and they'd all been arrested and threatened with trial for treason. Some said they should go to prison for the rest of the war. Others threatened to kill them. John Kline told the prisoners to stand firm, and eventually they were released. The prisoners had written many stanzas to the song while they were imprisoned, but John Kline had written the chorus.

"I think your great-aunt Anna thinks about your great-uncle John a lot, but she doesn't know how to talk about it. So today she sang a song. And tomorrow she might tell a story. And the next day? Who knows?"

***

Michael Kline thought back to 1846, a lifetime ago. John Kline was gone visiting. He was always gone visiting, riding his horse Nell north, south, east, and west. He doctored with his herbs and his plasters. And he preached and taught and helped to settle disagreements among the Brethren. He was always welcome everywhere he went.

Of course, when John was gone there was plenty of work to be done at the farm, and he and Anna had no children to help. But the Brethren always took care of each other. So if Elder Kline was out preaching, then it was up to all the rest of them at the Linville Creek congregation to share the chores at the farm. That's how it was done.

But Michael couldn't forget that day...

"Auntie," he called out. "Tante Anna! Are you home?"

The cart was in the yard and the horse was in the barn, but there was no answer.

"Hello!" he called out again.

Then he heard a small sound, as if someone was crying very far away. The house was not large. He found Anna Kline lying on the floor next to her bed. She was holding a letter in her hand.

"Daut is dead! Daut is dead!" she wept.

"What? How did he die?" Michael had asked, taking the letter from her hand. Everyone called John Kline "Daut."

"Daut is dead! What will we do?"

Frantically Michael read the letter.

"Tante Anna!" he pleaded. "John wrote this letter himself. He is not dead! It's in his handwriting. He is writing from Ohio to tell us that he is very ill, but that with our prayers he will recover."

But it was no use. Anna remained convinced that he was dead and gone. Not even when word came that he was recovering nor when he returned looking weak but very much alive could she be fully convinced.

And every time John had to go out on another trip Anna would insist that he was dead.

***

"At school the boys and girls say she's crazy," said Elizabeth. She wanted to finally get to the bottom of this, hoping her offering of pie would help. "My teacher says she has been crazy forever."

"She's not crazy," Michael replied with a little anger. But he knew that his Aunt Anna was not well, that she had never been well nearly as long as he had known her.

"She had a hard life," he continued. "You have to under-stand that she and your uncle planned to be a normal Brethren family with lots of children."

"What happened?"

"They had a son who died when he was very young and a daughter who died before birth. And after that, they didn't have any more children. It was very sad, very hard for them and for all of us."

"There are people in the town who still hate Uncle; they say he was a bad man."

"But what do the brothers and the sisters in the meeting-house say?" Michael asked.

"You know, you go to meetinghouse with me,"
said Elizabeth.

"Yes, but I want to hear you say it," Michael insisted.

"They say he was the greatest man who ever lived. They say that he was much loved everywhere."

"And what else?" Michael continued.

"That he was a martyr."

Then Michael and Elizabeth were interrupted.

"Please, it's the corn. Someone must bring in the corn!"

"That's Aunt Anna," he exclaimed as he rose from his chair and hurried to her bedroom. Elizabeth followed. The room was very crowded, for the family had moved most of John Kline's things in there. His old medicine cabinet was locked so that Aunt Anna would not get into it. His chair, with a very wide right arm that allowed plenty of room on which to rest a book, was in the corner just beyond the bed. And there was an old sundial right outside the window. John had made it and always used it to check his watch by it. If the watch and the sundial disagreed, Kline would change his watch.

There, on the edge of the bed, Anna Kline sat, a thin, frail old woman. She was rocking back and forth, one hand rubbing the other. Her eyes were closed.

"The corn! The corn! Who will harvest the corn?"

"Don't worry, Auntie. I will harvest the corn," Michael said.

"And I'll help," Elizabeth added, taking her hands. Michael kissed Anna on the forehead and the two waited. Slowly Anna Kline stopped rocking. They helped her back under the covers and she soon began to breathe deeply.

"I think she's asleep again," Elizabeth said at last.

***

Michael paused before leaving the room as he recalled those years when his uncle was so concerned for Anna.

"Is Anna okay?" John Kline asked. Michael had ridden out to meet him, and the two were riding back home together. There was a well-worn path and the horses knew it well, well enough that the two riders were able to relax. At times the woods hemmed them in closely and they rode single file, but for the most part they rode side by side in the sun.

"She is the same. Abram and Elizabeth Knopp tell me she has some good days, when she plays with their children," Michael answered. "You chose well when you asked them to live on the farm while you are gone."

"When my traveling days are over, I won't have to find people to take care of her. I will do it."

"When will your traveling days be over?" Michael asked him.

"When the Lord tells me they are over. Or when the Lord calls me home," John responded.

Michael had been hearing that sort of talk more and more frequently. He knew his uncle was aware that there were many who hated him. Anyone who stood against slavery was very unpopular.

"So how did you find Albemarle County?" Michael asked.

"There were very few Brethren. Mostly Baptists and Methodists. But those who are poor are always ready to hear the gospel. We have much in common with them. I feel that the Lord did well in sending me there."

"And what about the others?"

John Kline sighed. "There is one barrier between us and the wealthy classes that will continue, God only knows how long; and that barrier is slavery. The people who own slaves seem good in every other way, but they use the Bible to justify this horrible practice. The devil has blinded their eyes and their ears, and when you explain the Bible to them they do not understand."

Michael could tell his uncle was very upset. "What's the matter, John?" he asked.

John Kline shook his head. "I spoke to a man who travels much in the South. He told me a story of a family that was sold in North Carolina. The two young sons went to one owner, the daughter to another, and the mother to a third. Oh, what crying, what weeping, for never in their lives will they see each other again. I wonder, Michael. We Brethren do not practice war ourselves, but the stain of sin is so deep in our land, can it possibly be cleansed except with blood?"

No one could stop John Kline very long from traveling off to minister, to doctor, or just to visit— not even when they pleaded with him to stay closer to home because Anna wasn't doing well.

***

Michael was shaken from his thoughts. Elizabeth, who had gone for more pie, was shouting, "Grandfather! Tante Anna is gone!"

Michael ran to Anna's bedroom and found it empty, just like Elizabeth said.

"Don't worry. I'll find her!" he called as he ran out into the yard.

He was certain that she could not go far. Though she seemed very weak, every now and then Anna seemed to find the strength to walk away, just as she used to do so many years ago.

There she was. Crumpled up in a heap near the flower beds, unmoving. For a moment Michael Kline stood over her.

Sometimes, when he was very tired and it seemed like Aunt Anna was more trouble than usual, he wondered what it would have been like if his Uncle John had lived and been around more for Aunt Anna.

And then he asked himself, What if John Kline had never left home? What if he had ignored God's call? What if he and Aunt Anna had been given a large family? Where would the Brethren be then?

"Aunt Anna?" he asked.

But she said nothing. He bent over and picked her up. He was getting older himself, but she was light as light. Taking a deep breath, Michael Kline carried her back to her bed.

"See, Elizabeth. She's all right. Now before your mama comes for you, I want that other piece of pie!"

***

"What was the greatest thing that John Kline ever did?" Elizabeth asked, as her grandfather finished his pie.

Michael twirled his fork, trying to pick up the last crumbs of crust in the fruit that was smeared around his plate. He thought for a moment.

"Your great-uncle did so many important things, but I think the most important thing was the way he kept us together in unity during the Civil War. We Brethren in the South were in danger all the time, and most of the Brethren in the North did not come to visit us. It was too dangerous, and they had their own problems.

"It was dangerous for Uncle John, too, but he kept crossing the border between the South and the North. Even when he was warned that people were gunning for him, he kept traveling. He went to Annual Meeting. They made him the moderator. He preached everywhere, and he preached the same thing whether he was in Indiana or Ohio or Virginia or Maryland or North Carolina. He just never seemed to be afraid. He even told me how he had helped a deserter who had broken his leg."

"If he were still alive, do you think he could have kept the Brethren together?" Elizabeth asked.

Michael Kline sighed. In the past few years, the Brethren had split into three different churches. Differences over Sunday schools, missions, paying ministers, the way the love feast was observed, and many other things had split the Brethren apart. Some said the Brethren weren't changing fast enough, and others believed that nothing should ever change.

"Elizabeth, if John Kline were still alive, I think we'd still be one church."

"I wish he was still here," Elizabeth said. "If he were, I know he would give me a piece of candy, and I would give him a big hug."

"Me too," Michael said, remembering the day John Kline died as if it were yesterday.

***

"Don't go, Michael! They'll shoot you too!"

His wife was holding his arm, but Michael was putting on his black coat and walking to the door. The news was still fresh. The neighbor's boy had run in, telling them that the shots they'd all heard a couple of hours before had been bushwhackers. They had shot John Kline. He was dead. He was over on the hill, near the ridge, and no one had gone to get his body. No one was sure who else they would shoot.

Michael could guess who did it. The county was full of cowards, men who had neither gone bravely to war, nor stood bravely against war. They'd found an excuse for their own cowardice, an old injury perhaps, and now they were the sort who spent time in town leaning on the walls to hold them up, and always criticizing others.

Michael had also known that sooner or later they would plot in their cowardice to find a safe hiding place so that three or four or five or even more of them could safely shoot an old man on a horse who would do nothing to resist them.

"Don't go, Michael!" he heard again, but he hitched up the cart, and he went. He drove at a brisk pace. It was hard for the horses to get up that steep hill so he made sure they had a little speed before they climbed.

Long before he could see the crumpled form on the ground, Michael could hear John's horse, Nell, champing and neighing in her grief. Perhaps it would have been smarter to take a good long look to make sure no one was hiding behind a tree waiting to take another shot. Michael realized he didn't care. Let them shoot. He did not believe they had the courage to stay and wait. Killing unarmed old men was the limit of their bravery.

Quickly Michael laid out a sheet. He rolled his uncle over so that his body was lying on it. Then he stood up.

John Kline was smiling in death. Michael scratched his head.

"Just like you, John," he said aloud. "You have finished your race. You have won the prize. The rest of us are just starting to run. We're just starting."

Once the body was wrapped in the sheet, Michael placed his uncle in the back of the wagon and headed back down the hill. On the way up no one had spoken to him.

Now neighbors met him along the road. "We heard the shots. We thought someone was shooting squirrels for dinner."

Michael said nothing. Everyone had known this would happen. Now no one wanted to take the blame.

***

"Goodbye, Grandfather! Goodbye, Grandmother!" Elizabeth shouted as she left with her mother. "I'll see you tomorrow. Tell Tante Anna goodbye for me."

"So what did you and your grandfather talk about today?" Michael heard her mother ask as they rode away on the cart. And though he could not hear Elizabeth's reply, he knew it would have something to do with John Kline.

Maybe Elizabeth's mother would say nothing, but more than likely she would say something about how he was the greatest Brethren who had lived. Michael didn't know if that was true. But he knew that the story wasn't over. It was still going on. It was still going on in that quiet room where his aunt was sleeping—he hoped. And it was still going on in all those who cared for others. It was still going on for the ones who spoke the truth, no matter what it cost them. It was still going on.

Michael waved as the cart disappeared into the growing darkness. Then he turned back into the house to see how Aunt Anna was doing.

⚜

John Kline was murdered on June 15, 1864. His murderers were never tried, even though it was well known in the area who had killed him. Anna Kline died on May 4, 1885. They are both buried in the cemetery at the Linville Creek Church of the Brethren.

16
Saved from the Fire!

Abraham Harley Cassel

1890, Harleysville, Pennsylvania

"Cider later, fire first. Let's get things ready for to-night's bonfire. How does that sound, Caleb?"

Caleb Blake took a deep breath of the morning autumn air blowing through the bare branches. There was a bite to it. Only a few weeks ago, the fields had been filled with wheat,

blowing in the breeze like waves on a brown sea. When the occasional deer walked through the fields, it looked as if it were swimming.

Now the fields reminded Caleb of losing a tooth. For the longest time, the loose tooth was the most important thing in his life, wriggling only a little at first, but finally wobbling back and forth until one day, to his surprise, it would wrench itself free. Then his tongue would push back and forth against the bare spot, bothered more by the absence of the tooth than the presence of the pain.

Caleb was amazed by the empty fields. So much work, so fast, and suddenly real freedom.

Caleb didn't tell his pap that one of the reasons he looked forward to the bonfire and the cider was that it meant he could return to school. Pap didn't think much of school, and if there was work to do, he kept Caleb home. Not that his pap was cruel. It was just that Pap didn't think there was much use to learning if a boy was going to grow up to be a farmer.

"That sounds great, Pap!" he said aloud. "Can I help you unload the cart?"

"That's what I was hoping you'd say," Pap replied. The horse was waiting patiently as Pap jumped down from the cart and reached in to hand his son an armful of wood.

First the sticks, the bark, and the smaller branches. They were always at the heart of the great fire. There were plenty of big logs in the cart to be tossed on as well, Caleb was sure, but first his pap must get the kindling ready.

Old boxes, rotting wood, dried fir branches from a tree—all these were dumped in their turn. "This'll get the fire going good," Pap said.

"What's this?" Caleb asked suddenly, as Pap handed him a stack of old books.

"What's what?" Pap answered, as he pulled a stack of old newspapers from the cart.

"These books. The newspapers. Where did you get them? Why are we burning them?"

Pap laughed. "They're part of what was left in the attic after we had the sale on your uncle's place. After we buried him, the auction at his farm brought in a pretty penny, didn't it!"

"I don't remember seeing these books at the auction," Caleb commented, trying not to sound upset. He knew that was the surest way to get his pap, well, concerned.

"We only sold the useful things. Who would want these books? These are old books. Same with the newspapers. They're not even in English that a body could read if he chose to. These are in German jabber talk."

Pap dumped the load in his arms onto the ground near the kindling and reached in for a second batch.

"Wasn't Uncle a Dunker?"

"He was something or other, that's for sure. Dressed funny. Not like the rest of us in the family. Anyway, we don't have any room for this stuff, and I'm sure it's not worth anything. It might as well burn. They're all of no use. Not to you. Not to me."

Caleb knew he had to say something—and say it quickly. So he burst out: "I might want to read them someday."

"What?" Pap looked puzzled. "When are you going to read German? or read anything besides in school?"

"Pap—"

"Son, I have never known anything useful to come from a book that you couldn't learn on your own in the workshop or out in the field."

"Oh, please," Caleb suddenly pleaded, "please don't throw them in the fire, Pap. Brother Cassel says we must save these for the future."

Pap suddenly looked very puzzled. "Who is Brother Cassel, and what does he have to do with us?"

"He's got the big farm out near Harleysville, the one you talked about when we drove by a couple of times," explained Caleb.

"The one with the neat rows? That old fellow knows how to crack the whip, in a manner of speaking, when it comes to keeping his workers on the straight and narrow."

"He doesn't use a whip, Pap," Caleb said.

"I didn't mean he really uses a whip. But where did you meet this man? You're always with me on the farm."

"At school. He came to our school and showed us old books. He's got books older than America. He's got more books than a library. And he's a farmer, too. He told us you should never throw away a book or a newspaper or a magazine. Not until you find out if it is worth something."

"What do you mean, worth something?" Pap asked, scratching his head. "Like money?"

"Maybe," Caleb admitted.

Pap reached into the cart and pulled out another stack of books, then paused.

"This is something you really want to do, Caleb?"

His son nodded. "A lot."

"I can't see that there's any use to these books and papers and things, but if you will take it over to Mr. Cassel and get it out of my way this instant, I'll let it go."

"Can I drive the cart?" Caleb asked excitedly.

Pap smiled. "I suppose so. Now there's a ton of this stuff—you be careful."

"I will!" The boy leaned over and lifted a stack of the books toward his father, who was putting back the things he had already gathered.

Pap paused. "You know what, Caleb? I'm going with you. I'm going to get my money's worth from this Mister Cassel."

"Okay," Caleb replied, with a little less excitement in his voice. "But can I still drive the cart?"

Pap laughed. "Yes, son. You bet. It's about time. And let's hurry. I want to get back in time to have the bonfire tonight."

Over the hill and down the road the two traveled. Caleb was anxious to show his father that he could handle the reins; he was probably far more careful than he would have been if he'd been driving by himself, but Pap seemed to enjoy looking around at the other farms, where there were still oats and barley to be harvested.

"I think we're getting close," Caleb said, as they passed by a field of winter wheat, lush and green in contrast to the brown, drying corn or the bare trees.

"Maybe that's him!" Caleb pointed to an old man in black clothes. He wore heavy work boots, and a broad black hat. His long white beard drooped from his chin to the second or third button of his shirt.

"You can do better," they overheard the man calling out to one of the workers in his field. "I want to see more work."

"That's the way to run a farm," Pap said with approval as they drew up alongside.

"Pardon me!" Caleb called. "Are you Mr. Cassel?"

The old man looked up at them from beneath the brim of his hat. "Ja," he admitted. "I am Abraham Harley Cassel. And how can I help you today?"

"The lad has some books in the back of the cart, which he thinks you might be interested in," Pap said, gesturing over his shoulder. "He thinks they might be worth something."

At the mention of books, the old man's eyes widened and a broad smile filled out the rest of his face above the beard.

"Books? Did you say books?" Abraham held out his hand, and when Pap took it, he lifted himself up to the buckboard and sat between the two. "Take me to the house and we'll have a look at these." He then pointed to the worker whom he'd been scolding. "You walk over to the house, you hear? You can help unload the books from this cart and do some good work today, right?"

He then turned to Pap. "It's been years since I turned the farm over to my son, but I cannot help myself. I still watch over the workers to see that they do an honest day's labor."

"I like the way you run the farm," Pap said. "No nonsense and hard work. Maybe you can talk to my son, Caleb, here."

"And what would you want me to tell him?" Abraham asked.

"Tell him how important hard work is," Pap said. "He always talks about reading books and going to school, but farm work comes first, and he needs to know that."

"Congratulations!" Abraham said with a smile. "You could not say it better."

Caleb was puzzled. What was Mr. Cassel saying? But he was not through speaking.

"Congratulations. You are saying exactly the right things to make sure your boy treasures books and becomes a collector like me," Mr. Cassel continued.

"What?" Pap asked.

"My father was a good man, sir, but he did his best to make sure I never got to read. Schooling?" Abraham laughed. "I went only six weeks. Always farm work, harder and harder. And I was a hard worker, sir. But I read by candlelight at night when the work was done, and I was so tired I could hardly keep my eyes open. Then my father would stop me when I would go to bed with a lighted candle, so I took to hiding matches in my room."

"Oh," was all Pap could say.

"And when I could buy books of my own, I did. I never threw away a book, either. Later I became a teacher and I would visit the parents of my students. They would let me look in their attics and in the tool sheds. Old books, old papers. I kept them all."

They pulled up to the house. "Here we are. Come inside. Hello, Elizabeth. We have company."

"How is my book fool today?" said the cheerful woman who met them at the door. "Welcome, come inside. You come to look at the books, yes?"

"She was a Quaker when I met her, but she is a good Brethren now," Abraham explained as they entered together. The house was dark to their eyes that were used to the light outside. He led them to a flight of stairs and into a long room.

It was everything Caleb imagined. Down the long room were drawers up to a height of three feet, and above them bookshelves to the ceiling, crammed with books. A long table filled most of the available space, with more books stacked every which way.

"These are all your books?" Caleb asked. "This is more than a library."

Abraham chuckled. "This isn't even half of them. There's another room just like this, and still more. My wife is very patient."

Pap's mouth was wide open.

"Have you read all these books?" he asked.

"What is the use of having a book if you cannot read it? Listen, sir, each one of these books is the work of a man or a woman. Some are very learned. Some have hardly been to school. But here in these pages are their lives and their thoughts and their dreams and their hopes. Here is something they thought was worth saying. I am just one person, but with these books, I learn about many. I go many places around the world that I never travel to."

"But it's not the same as going there, is it?" Pap asked.

Abraham shrugged. "Maybe not. But I can't go back to talk to Jesus Christ, can I? Yet in the pages of the Bible, I meet him. And, of course, many people, not the same as Jesus, but those who have struggled with the same things I have."

"Well, maybe you have a point," Pap said, "but you can find these books at the colleges, right? You don't have to own them."

Abraham shook his head. "No, some of these books are nowhere else. Can you believe it? People throw books out. They burn them. They do not save them. They always think someone else will keep a copy. There are books here about many things, including our own history as a Dunker church—some that exist nowhere else. Now people come to me, a man with only six weeks of schooling, to ask me questions, to look at my books, to learn. And they tell me things and I learn from them. You never stop learning, you know."

"I guess you're right, Mr. Cassel," Pap said.

"Ah, here come your books," Abraham interrupted, as his worker entered the room, huffing and puffing, with a stack of books and papers. "Lay them right here."

"There's more," the man grumbled.

"Then go get them. Dinner is soon and you don't want to miss it, right?"

Carefully the old man began to unstack the books.

"Where did you get these books?"

"From my uncle's house—John Garber."

"I saw the flier for the estate sale," Abraham said, "but it didn't mention books. Why were these not purchased then?"

"We didn't try to sell them."

"Look here," Cassel said, excited, "here is a copy of *The Defense of Baptism* by John Kline. I do not have more than a copy or two of this book. And look here, the sermon by Brother John Bowman on temperance. These books in German, very nice, some volumes of the writings of Martin Luther."

"So the books are worth something?" Caleb asked.

"Yes, yes. And these papers, the *Christian Family Companion* and *Der Evangelische Besuch*. All of these, much needed. And this, a hymnal. And that, over there, a book of proverbs for children. There are things I do not have. Oh good, put those things over here," he instructed the man as he entered with a second load of books and papers.

At that moment, Elizabeth Cassel called from below, "Abraham, there's someone else to see you."

As the man came into the room, Abraham welcomed him and turned to Caleb and his pap. "Please, let me introduce you to a great educator and a member of the Brethren,

Martin Grove Brumbaugh." The man was neatly dressed and without the Brethren beard, Caleb was surprised to see.

"Pleased to meet you," Brumbaugh said. "I'm sorry to interrupt. If you are busy I can wait. I only came to ask you some questions about the feetwashing." He turned to face Pap and Caleb. "This man is helping me write my book. I am working on the first history of our church, and without him, I could not write a word. So much he has saved, so much he has preserved. Our history and our heritage is preserved right here on these shelves. Can you imagine?"

"You're writing a book?" Pap said, with a great deal of surprise and shock.

"With the help of Abraham Harley Cassel, the greatest bookman of this age."

"Well, let me tell you, Brother Martin, that the controversy about the feetwashing is easily solved, though some will not allow themselves to look at the facts. It is clear that the mother church in Germantown practiced the single mode of feetwashing, where one brother washes the feet of the man next to him, and that brother washes the feet of the man next to him, and so on. But those who champion the double mode are ignoring the testimony of the writings and the testimony of those I have spoken to of the ancient Brethren."

"Tell them about Brother D. P. Sayler," Brumbaugh said, with a smile.

"Yes, yes. Brother Sayler believes I am wrong, but a committee sent him to my library to hear what I had to say. When Brother Sayler arrived, he learned that I was not here, but at a love feast. So he came to the library by himself, walked up and down the length, and then left, even though he was begged to remain until I returned. Then he went back to the committee and told them that he had been through the library of Abraham Harley Cassel and he had found nothing to contradict his view."

Abraham laughed heartily and went on. "But Brother Martin, as it turns out, I have just the thing for you. Today this young man, Caleb, brought me another copy of this number of the *Christian Family Companion* for April 9, 1872. And what is in these pages? My own little letter on the history of the feetwashing. I am not a good writer, not having any education to speak of, but I think this will answer your questions."

Then Abraham turned to Caleb and Pap. "But first let me talk to these two. These books you bring, how much money do you want to sell them for? I will buy the books, all of them."

"No you won't," Pap continued as Caleb looked up in surprise. "You heard me. I'm not going to sell you the books. You've taught me something today—that books are pretty valuable. I think I will be sending Caleb to school now, even in harvest. The books are yours, Mr. Cassel, and good luck to you."

Abraham shook his hand heartily. "Thank you, thank you, sir. But you won't leave here empty-handed. First of all, Caleb, I'm putting this book in your hands. It is a book of science, one that I already have, that tells us about the planets that circle the sun. The Lord has made a wonderful creation that extends far beyond this humble soil of Pennsylvania."

"Thank you!" Caleb said.

"And you sir," Abraham continued, "I have something for you as well. You had a very nice load of wood in the back of that cart. I was thinking of having a nice fire for the workers tonight. What can I pay you for that load of wood?"

Abraham Harley Cassel, who died in 1908, did more than anyone else to preserve Brethren history in the nineteenth century. Most of his collection is at Juniata College in Pennsylvania, where you can see some of it today. People come from all over the world to read his books.

Martin Grove Brumbaugh, who later became governor of Pennsylvania, published his history of the Church of the Brethren in 1899.

17
The Meanest Man in Patrick County

Cain Lackey

1892, Patrick County, Virginia
"Whoa," said Brother W. A. Elgin, as he pulled on the arm of Brother J. A. Dove. "You don't want to go down there if you can help it!"

"Why?" asked Brother Dove, a little puzzled. He could hear the fear in his companion's voice.

Both men were Brethren ministers. They wore dark coats and white shirts. They had long beards with no mustaches. But both men wore heavy boots, because, like many Brethren ministers, they were also farmers and worked in the fields.

Brother Elgin was showing Brother Dove the sights of Patrick County, Virginia. Brother Dove had come to preach a

revival at Smith River Church near Elamsville, where
Brother Elgin was pastor.

Why should he be frightened, he wondered as he looked
down into the swamp? All he could see was a young man digging a ditch. The man looked very strong and was working
hard.

"That's Cain Lackey," Brother Elgin replied. "You have
to be very careful around him. He is the meanest man in
Patrick County."

The year was 1892 and Patrick County, Virginia, was a
place of dirt fields and mud roads. Folks were strong and
they worked hard to make a living, but they didn't always
have enough to eat. When the flu came through, a lot of people died. Brother Dove was learning that there were plenty
of places in Patrick County you couldn't get to most of the
year because the roads were so bad. Even though people
loved Jesus and loved to go to church, many of them
couldn't get to a church, no way, no how.

Despite all the hardship, he found the area very beautiful
there in the Blue Ridge Mountains, where winding rivers
raced over the boulders in their streambeds. And in the
western part of the county, he had seen the rich fields of
corn, tobacco, and buckwheat, and the long grasses that fed
cattle, sheep, and horses. There were dairy farms, and there
were orchards so plentiful that the smell of the fruit was like
the winds of perfume. Indeed, the fruit of Patrick County
was shipped throughout the state, and people spoke highly
of its goodness. There was so much that was rich and full in
Patrick County.

But here in Elamsville life was difficult, and Brother Dove wanted to tell people how much Jesus loved them, to give them hope and to encourage them to continue to love each other and help each other. Folks tried hard to make ends meet, but life was so desperate for some that they ended up in the poorhouse, unable to take care of themselves and dependent on the charity of others.

"Well, he certainly looks like the strongest man in the county," Brother Dove said, watching the way Cain Lackey thrust his shovel into the swamp, sending great splatters of mud into the air behind him.

"That he is," Brother Elgin said. "No one can work like him. He's so strong that he can carry around a railroad tie the way most men carry a two-by-four. Around here he's known as one of the roughest and most ignorant mountaineers that ever shouldered an ax. And he can wrestle something fierce. They say even when he was a pup there were big men who could throw him on the ground, but no one could make him stay there."

"Lots of folks wrestle, but that doesn't make them mean. So why do you say he is the meanest man in the county?" Brother Dove asked.

"Around these parts they still talk about the big fight with the feller they call Champion Ben," Brother Elgin said. "This place is full of mountain men and bootleggers who make illegal whiskey. It's rough country, and the law doesn't come here very often to settle things, so folks settle things themselves. You ever heard of Jeb Stuart?" Brother Elgin asked.

Brother Dove nodded. "The Confederate general. He came from these parts, didn't he?"

"Born right here in Patrick County," Brother Dove said proudly. "We're famous for him here. But Champion Ben was even more famous than Jeb Stuart. He could lick any man, fighting fair *or* dirty. When he came through here a couple of years ago with his cronies, a pretty tough bunch themselves, he said he would take on any challengers who weren't afraid to face him. No one would. So Champion Ben started saying bad things about the folks around here. Then in walked Cain Lackey. The place got real quiet. Cain said he'd meet Champion Ben over by the river, unless he was scared."

"What happened?"

"What happened was he laid that Champion Ben low with a single blow. And when Champion Ben got up, then Cain would hit him again. So those thirteen companions of Champion Ben tried to pull Cain away. It was no good. He beat them up, too. Finally, they took some mule spurs, you know, those sharp spurs you wear on your boots to make a mule mind—and it takes a lot to make a mule mind—and they hacked Cain with them, until finally he stepped back. Then they all ran away, clear out of the county, because they were so scared of Cain Lackey. He's still got the scars, Cain does, but it hasn't tamed him. Everyone's scared of him. I'm scared of him."

Cain Lackey stopped working and shouldered his shovel. He stood nearly knee-deep in the trench he had dug and was looking up at the two ministers. Brother Dove hefted his heavy Bible. His mouth was suddenly dry. Was he afraid, too, he wondered? Maybe he was.

"A man like that must have had a tough childhood," he said.

"Yep," Brother Elgin agreed. " I blame his father. By the age of ten he was working the plow same as any man. His daddy made him sleep under the open sky during the summer so he could get right to work when the sun came up. He would wake up with his clothes soaked with dew, but he could work more than any ten grown men.

"When he was just a boy, his daddy made him build a mill all by himself. That's man's work, but Cain did it. All the cutting and the sawing and the planning and the hammering. That mill still runs today there by the river. Folks talk about it. Even though his daddy took all the credit, everyone knew it was Cain who built it.

"There was no time for playing for that boy. Just hard work and hard times. He can't read or write. Fighting's mostly what he knows."

"I'm going to invite him to the revival," Brother Dove said suddenly, taking a step down toward Cain Lackey. He could see the big man stiffen, as if he felt threatened.

"He'll never come," Brother Elgin said.

"He'll definitely never come if we don't ask him," Brother Dove replied. "He's the very man I want to see, because Christ came to save sinners. Those who have not had a good earthly father need to know that they have a Father in heaven who loves them."

Brother Dove took a few steps, then stopped and turned. "Wait here for me."

"I will," Brother Elgin said. "If there's any trouble, I'll send for help. A lot of it."

"There won't be any trouble. You wait and see."

So Brother Elgin watched as the Brethren minister

descended into the swamp. Brother Elgin could see Brother
Dove step first ankle-deep and then knee-deep into the
swamp, getting mud and gunk all over him. He watched as
Brother Dove stuck out his hand to Cain Lackey. After a
moment Cain took his hand.

Brother Elgin winced. He knew that Cain had a grip of
iron. Other folks told him so. But Brother Dove didn't flinch.

They were talking, Brother Elgin could see that, but he
couldn't hear them. Any moment he expected to see Cain
Lackey raise a fist and lay Brother Dove low into the mud,
and then he'd have to decide if he wanted to run in and save
him. Brother Elgin was afraid, but he had decided that's
exactly what he would do, run in and save Brother Dove, but
the longer he watched the later it became and still no trouble.

Brother Dove was opening his Bible and cradled it on one
arm while raising another. Cain Lackey seemed to tense up,
and he raised one of his arms just a bit, but that was it. Cain
cocked his head to one side, and it looked to Brother Elgin
that Cain was really listening.

Then they were shaking hands again, and Brother Dove
was walking back to him. Mud clung to his boots and pants
and he climbed back up to the road.

"What did he say?" Brother Elgin asked. Cain Lackey had
already returned to digging. Not much seemed to keep him
from work.

"He said he'd come to the revival," Brother Dove replied.
"Is he as good as his word?"

"Yes. If he tells you he'll come, he'll be there. He's just that
way. He'll do what he tells you. But if he tells you he'll give
you a whipping, he'll do that, too."

The church was full that night at the revival. People had come from miles around to hear Brother Dove. There were young people and old people, children and mothers and fathers and aunts and uncles, grandmothers and grandfathers, and a few babies and a few great-grandparents who packed themselves into the church. All the windows were open, but it was still hot inside, but no one left. When someone like Brother Dove came to preach, it was something special, very special.

A sweaty man in the front of the church was moving his arms up and down, right and left, directing the singing. Everyone already knew the songs, which was a good thing, because there weren't enough songbooks for everyone.

They sang songs about the blood of Jesus and songs about the good things Jesus did and songs about heaven and dying and a great trumpet shout. There were songs about angels and songs about the cross and songs about the love of God and the power of the Holy Spirit.

Everyone loved the songs and they especially loved the fact that there was somewhere to go that night. Even though there was plenty of hard work that would come early the next morning for everyone, people stayed. The hard work would always be there. A revival like this might last two or three nights, or it might last a week, from Sunday to Sunday, but then there wouldn't be another revival for a year or more, unless folks heard about one the next county over.

Everyone had folks staying in their homes, relatives and friends and total strangers. There were people sleeping in extra bedrooms, but most of the people were poor and didn't have extra bedrooms, so people slept in the hay that was scattered in the barns, up in the lofts. Kids loved to stay in the haylofts with their friends and relatives, their cousins and second cousins, and folks that were no kin at all.

There were people sleeping in attics and in bedrolls under the stars, beneath the shelter of the branches. If rain came, they'd all wake up and everyone would make room for them in the houses.

People were even planning to sleep in the church that night, on the church floor, on the benches and under the benches, up in the church loft, and outside under the eaves. They ate together, sharing what little food they had. There was the smell of cooking in the air, and even a rumor that there might be ice cream one of these nights, because there were always enough hands to turn the crank of the ice cream maker.

Brother Dove looked out over the congregation. Some folks he recognized and some he didn't. Everyone was there, everyone but Cain Lackey.

Then the singing was over, and it was time for Brother Dove to get up and preach. He took a deep breath. He was planning to preach a good long time. There was no telling how long he might preach, and no one particularly cared, because they loved preaching. In those days if you wanted to hear the Word of God, then you went to the church to hear it. If you wanted to hear music, then people had to sing it for you.

Brother Dove took another deep breath, and then he saw a big man standing in the doorway of the church. It was Cain Lackey all right, and he had a child in his arms. Brother Dove hadn't thought about it, but now he knew that Cain Lackey was married and had children. By then there was no more room for anyone else in the church, but when Cain came in the door, people made room for him to sit down because they were afraid of him.

Opening his Bible, Brother Dove began to read and to talk. He spoke about the love Jesus has for those who are lost. He told about the tax collector who was afraid to raise his eyes when he prayed, and how Jesus said God loved that sinner. He told about the prodigal son, who wasted the money his father gave him, but who was still welcomed back home when he returned penniless and starving from a distant country.

Brother Dove told about the Apostle Paul, who had hunted down Christians in order to arrest them and send them to their deaths, and how Jesus found Paul and turned him around so that he took the good news about Jesus throughout the Roman Empire. Brother Dove talked about the Old Testament prophets who told the people what was wrong in their lives but also made it clear that God was giving them another chance to change.

It got hotter and hotter in the building, and Brother Dove was dripping with sweat, and so was everyone else. It had gotten dark outside, and it was getting dark in the church as well. He could barely see into the back row. And he wondered, What did Cain Lackey, the meanest man in Patrick County, think about what he was saying?

And finally Brother Dove talked about the thief who was crucified next to Jesus, who stood up for Jesus when others made fun of him and said that Jesus did not deserve what was happening to him.

"The thief asked Jesus to remember him when he came into his kingdom," Brother Dove said, "and Jesus told him, 'Truly, I say to you, today you will be with me in Paradise.'

If Jesus could save the thief on the cross, then Jesus can save you from your sins as well."

Brother Dove asked the people to sing one more song, a song about accepting Jesus, a song about coming forward so all could pray over the sinners:

Softly and tenderly Jesus is calling, calling for you and for me.
See, on the portals he's waiting and watching,
    watching for you and for me.
Come home, come home, ye who are weary, come home.
Earnestly, tenderly, Jesus is calling, calling, O sinner,
    come home.

Brother Dove said that he would be baptizing all those who came forward. The song went on and on, louder and louder. Some of the people were crying, some were squeezing forward so that Brother Dove and Brother Elgin and all the other Brethren ministers could pray for them. Sometimes they were so weak they could hardly stand. Many people were coming forward to accept Jesus.

But not Cain Lackey. Brother Dove could see a dark shadow, a silhouette of a man, standing at the back of the church. Cain Lackey was standing, but he could see there was no way Cain Lackey could come forward, even if he wanted to. The church was too packed.

Then he saw something that surprised him. Cain Lackey was standing on top of a church bench. He was holding the little girl in his arms, and she was fast asleep. This person who was supposed to be the worst person in Patrick County had a little girl asleep in his arms, and he was coming forward by walking on the tops of the church benches.

The other ministers stood back as if they were shocked, but Brother Dove welcomed Cain Lackey and hugged him very tight, him and his daughter, and then invited him to kneel while they prayed together. All along the singing continued. And then a cool breeze blew in the window, a breeze that brought relief and comfort.

When he was through praying, Brother Dove raised his hands and suddenly everyone was quiet. No one was singing. No one was crying. Everyone was listening.

"Today you have seen a miracle of grace," he said. "God has called this man to do great things, just like the Apostle Paul. You will be the ones who will see these things. Welcome this man into our church!"

But not everyone was glad to see Cain Lackey come forward. "This is the meanest man in Patrick County," some said. "How can we trust him?"

"The Bible tells us that the people didn't trust the Apostle Paul when he was first baptized," Brother Dove explained. "He had been putting Christians in jail, and people were afraid of him. But Barnabas stood up for him, and Paul became the greatest evangelist the world has ever known."

"But this isn't the Apostle Paul. It's Cain Lackey."

"Who knows what the Lord will do with this man. He may become a great evangelist as well," responded Brother Dove.

"If Cain Lackey is baptized and joins this church, we might just all leave," said someone else.

While the argument went on, some looked toward Cain Lackey and wondered if he might get mad because they were talking about him. If he got mad, he might lay one of them low with a single blow.

But Cain Lackey just hung his head and said, "I want to be baptized, but I will come to church until the people trust me."

People didn't trust him at first. Some thought he wouldn't change. Once, when he was coming to church, a ruffian tried to get him to fight just like in the old days, but Cain Lackey knew that Brethren didn't believe in fighting to get their way, so he told them, "Boys, I surrender. My hands are up. I refuse to fight." And he stared at the ruffian until he turned around and walked away.

Cain would say, "I believe in Jesus now. My life is changed. You'll see."

And the people did see. Cain Lackey was changed. It wasn't long before everyone saw the change and he was baptized, and what Brother Dove said came true. Cain Lackey became a great worker for Jesus!

Cain had never read a Bible, because he could not read. He had never heard the Bible read because no one opened the family Bible in his house. His father had told him he would never amount to much and did not send him to school or let him learn how to read.

Now, even though he was an adult and was worried that people would make fun of him, Cain Lackey learned to read. It was hard work. He had to rely on others to read for him, and to teach him. The book he loved to read most of all was the Bible! Now Cain knew his Heavenly Father loved him very much, and he wanted others like him to know this as well.

Soon Cain became a preacher, the most famous preacher in Patrick County. He started churches and brought many more people into those churches.

The churches Cain built are still standing. The children of the children of the people Cain Lackey baptized and his own children and children's children are still part of the Church of the Brethren. People remember Cain Lackey as a miracle of grace. They are not ashamed to claim Cain Lackey as their own, because he was no longer the meanest man in Patrick County.

He was God's servant, the greatest servant of God in Patrick County.

18
Never Give Up!

Julia Gilbert

1926, Ohio

"I want to play with Auntie Julia! I want to play with Auntie Julia!"

The little boy was crying, jumping up and down, his arms extended skyward. The little boy's mother arched an eyebrow. Another woman stood beside them.

"Oh," mother scolded,
but she was smiling as she spoke. "You wouldn't eat your breakfast, and then you made that fuss in front of all those people, and now you want to play with Aunt Julia?"

"I want to play with Auntie Julia!"

"Very well. But only if she wants to play with you."

There was little question of that. The little boy ran up the steps to the house where the eighty-two-year-old Julia Gilbert lived, taking care of several young children who belonged to a niece who had died eight years before. Before he could knock, the door swung open and the kindly woman greeted him with arms open wide.

"Well!" said the mother's companion. "You were right. That child loves his Auntie Julia. She seems good with kids. Did she have children of her own?"

"No," the mother replied. "She never married. She has always lived with relatives."

"Never married? Never had children of her own?" the woman asked skeptically. "I noticed that she walks rather strangely. Is something wrong with her."

Mother shrugged. "One leg is a good deal shorter than the other. When she was eleven years old, she nearly died from scarlet fever, which crippled her for life. Let's go in—you should meet her."

The woman arched her eyebrow. She didn't act as if she especially wanted to meet Julia Gilbert. "Well, I guess it's nice that she can help take of children, but really, has her life amounted to anything? No children, no husband, and always living with relatives. Wouldn't it have been kinder if she had died with that childhood disease?"

Mother paused. She didn't like what her friend was saying. But she gave her a firm reply: "Don't you know? That's Julia Gilbert! She's the woman who changed the Church of the Brethren—all by herself. I wish we were all as useless as she is!"

***

1855

"Mother, where are Ann and Jonas?"

Little Julia Gilbert was lying in her bed. She was running a high fever. Her face was red and covered with splotches. Her throat was sore and parched.

Her mother exchanged the wet rag on her forehead with a fresh one. Mother's eyes looked red and swollen, as if she had been crying.

"Please, Julia, just get some rest. Don't ask questions."

Father was standing next to Mother. He draped an arm around her shoulder.

"I'm sorry we came so far west, so far from doctors and medicines," he said in a quiet voice.

"Hush," mother said softly. "Not here, not in front of Julia."

Julia tried to look to her side but she was weak. And she was worried. She could not hear her brother and sister. There were no groans from their direction.

"I'm glad we came west," Mother continued. "There is more land here, more opportunity than back in Maryland. But there is also more danger. And God has seen fit to spare Julia."

"I wonder why," Father said. "Why is Julia alive and not...," but then he stopped himself before he said aloud what Julia would soon guess, that her sister Ann Zillah and her brother Jonas had died from the measles and the scarlet fever.

"I don't know why God has allowed the others to... leave us, but I am sure God has a special plan for Julia," Mother said. "She loves the Brethren. All she talks about is going to

Annual Meeting. I think God has something special for her to do. I just know it."

"I'm sure you're right," Father said.

***

1858

There were those who worried that the little girl with a limp would not be able to walk into the river when it was time for her to be baptized into the membership of the Wolf Creek Church, but Julia made it very clear that she was going into the waters by herself.

Few children read the Bible as much as she did, or knew as much about Brethren history and practice. She always had questions for the ministers after the worship on Sunday. And sometimes she would disagree with what the minister said about the Bible. Most of the time the ministers laughed at her, the little girl who walked with difficulty because one leg was much shorter than the other, but sometimes they found it hard to answer her questions.

The baptism itself was very exciting for Julia. Because it was not easy for her to walk, she stumbled in the river. Her heart pounded wildly, but the minister who was about to perform the baptism took her head.

"Don't be afraid, Julia. Jesus went here before."

That was right, she thought. Jesus had been baptized by John the Baptist. She was walking in the same steps as Jesus. She was still nervous and a little frightened, but as she knelt down, Julia thought to herself, "Dear God, I promise to you that I will live faithful to Jesus until I die."

Then she was dunked once, twice, three times in the rushing water. When she came up for the third time, she felt as if she had been changed for good.

The best thing, she knew, was that she could now take part in the feetwashing, the love feast, and the communion. When she was baptized, she had pledged to follow Jesus all her life. The love feast was a way of getting even closer to Jesus.

Julia always enjoyed the simplicity of the meetinghouse, but on the night of the love feast, it was transformed. The benches and tables were turned around, so that the meal could be shared in the church. The smell of the food from the church kitchen was rich and made Julia feel more hungry than she could remember.

"This is the meal I am sharing with Jesus," she thought to herself as she sat down at a bench next to her mother. The tables were bare as the ceremony of the feetwashing began. Afterwards the food was brought out to the table from the kitchen. Julia enjoyed eating the meat and the broth, with the thick pieces of bread soaking up all the flavor in the soup.

Then she watched as the elders passed a long piece of the communion bread to a man at the end of each table. After the man broke off a piece of the bread, he then passed it along to the next man who broke off a piece as well.

However, when the elders came to the side where the women sat, they held out the long strip of communion bread to a sister who broke off a piece. That sister did not break a piece of the bread with the next sister. Instead, the elder stepped down the line and held the bread for the rest of the women. That seemed odd. And something else bothered her, something she couldn't put her finger on.

That night after going to bed, Julia began to toss and turn. Something was wrong, but she could not figure out what was the matter. Suddenly Julia sat up, lit a candle, and found her Bible.

Everything had seemed perfect at the love feast, but something was nagging her, something to do with the Bible passage read at church. Quickly she thumbed through the pages until she found the Gospel of John. Her finger ran up and down the pages. There it was—chapter 13. She started to read, then stopped at verse 4: "He riseth from supper, and laid aside his garments; and took a towel, and girded himself."

Then she realized what it was. The Bible said that Jesus rose from supper and began the feetwashing. But at her love feast, the meal wasn't set on the tables until after the feetwashing.

At first Julia decided it didn't matter that much. Blowing out the candle, she went back to bed. But the next day she found she was still thinking about it, and the day after that. At last, on the third day following the love feast, Julia waited until her father was done with the chores and all the other hard work around the farm. He was sitting on a low rocking chair, relaxing and studying his own Bible while humming a hymn. Julia approached him with a Bible in her hand. And waited.

"What is it, Julia, my dear?" he asked at last. "Another question from the Bible?"

Julia read him the verse from John. Then she told him that supper should be laid on the tables before the feetwashing, and not after.

At first Father said nothing. He wrinkled up his forehead and cheeks and squinted his eyes as if trying to drill a hole in the pages. Then he looked up at Julia and slowly sighed.

"The old Brethren took the ordinance from several passages of Scripture and thought this was the proper way to do it."

Now it was Julia's turn to stand silent for a moment. She opened her Bible and shifted her weight a little; it was always uncomfortable for her to stand for long periods of time.

Finally she smiled and nodded her head. "Thank you, Father," she said, satisfied with his answer.

But she was satisfied only for a little while. A few days later she spoke with her father again, and then to a couple of the ministers on Sunday. One of them asked her why she was pursuing the point.

"When I was baptized, I made a vow to God to walk in all his ways and to read the scriptures," she said. "I believe it is our duty to do things the way Jesus taught us to do them."

Julia did not give up. She spoke with others at the church, asking their opinion, and inviting them to read the passage.

The next year at the love feast the supper was set out at the tables before the people came into the room to sit down for the feetwashing. No one said anything at the dinner about Julia's study of the Scriptures and her insistence that they do things the way it was written in the Bible. They didn't need to. Everyone knew.

***

1883, Wolf Creek, Ohio

Julia grew up to adulthood. Though she had no children of her own, she loved children. Families knew that they could bring their children to her and she would care for them. She was also quite busy working around the house, keeping things in order. As her mother and father grew older, she devoted a lot of time to taking care of them, too.

Julia continued to read her Bible and began to think long and hard about another practice of the love feast: the fact that the men broke bread with each other at the communion, but the women did not break bread—it was broken for them by a man.

Julia knew there had been no women present at the Last Supper, so the fact that the sisters took part in the love feast was something different from the Bible. But there was nothing in the Bible that suggested to her that if women were there they were to be treated differently.

In addition to studying her Bible, Julia also read the Brethren magazines that came to her parents' home. One day an article caught her eye. It was on the very subject she'd been thinking about—whether the sisters should be allowed to break bread with each other. The article was written by I. J. Rosenberger, a famous Brethren preacher and writer. Julia had heard him preach at Annual Meeting and was impressed by him.

But the article disappointed her. Brother Rosenberger gave some reasons why women should not break bread for themselves. First, they were not allowed to serve in the military. Next they were not allowed to be preachers. Also, in the Old Testament they were not allowed to enter into the inner court of the temple. Therefore, the writer felt that women were not to break bread in the communion.

Julia thought about it a long time but wasn't sure Brother Rosenberger's reasons made sense. If most Brethren men didn't serve in the military, so what did it matter if women did not? And Julia knew that there *were* some women among the Brethren who preached, women such as Mattie Dolby and Sarah Righter Major, even though not everyone approved. She had also heard they were very good preachers. And finally, what did it matter what happened in the temple? Didn't the Brethren follow Jesus, and not the old law?

Late that night Julia took her elderly mother aside. "Mother," Julia asked, trying not to laugh, "if this writer is correct, and women must have the bread broken for them, why stop there? If a man must break the bread for a woman, shouldn't a man also wash a woman's feet? And what about the holy kiss we share, where the men give the men a kiss and the women give the women a kiss? Should the men now kiss the women during communion?"

Julia's mother laughed out loud. "Julia, you are as clever as ever. I think you should write a letter to *The Gospel Messenger* and tell them this. But please, please, say it nicely. We don't want the beards to fall off all the good old Brethren, do you think?"

And Julia wrote that letter.

***

1894 Wolf Creek, Ohio

Every year all the Brethren met in a council meeting in their church to talk over the issues and settle problems. Julia's parents were now very old, but they came with her to the council meeting, because they knew she wanted to speak up this time.

"Is there anyone who has a question they want to send to the Annual Meeting?" asked the moderator of the church.

Julia stood up. She was a little nervous, but she kept her eyes on her paper and read out loud.

"Oh no, not that again," someone said, not very loudly, but loud enough for everyone to hear.

Julia pretended she didn't hear. "Dear Brethren," she read, "we, the sisters of the Wolf Creek Church, seeing that we have made the same covenant with God in Christ Jesus that you made, petition Annual Meeting through district meeting to repeal your former decisions against us and grant us the same privilege in the breaking of bread and passing the cup as you do the brethren."

Julia waited a moment, then sat down.

One of her neighbors finally stood up, a sturdy farmer with a long beard. "It seems to me that this was settled a long time ago by the elders. I don't see why we should trouble the Annual Meeting with it."

One of the women in the congregation answered, "But what if she is right? Let's let the Annual Meeting decide."

But the farmer shook his head. "How could she be right when all the elders disagree with her? It doesn't make sense."

Julia stood up, a little bit afraid. "Maybe there's only one of me saying this, and a lot of other folks saying otherwise, but we Brethren do not do something just because everyone else does it. We do things the way we do, because that's what it says in the Bible."

"That's right," another farmer said. "If the Bible agrees with her, then she's right, no matter what other folks say."

"Sounds like she convinced you!" snorted the first farmer.

The second farmer blushed. "That's not it at all, but I see no harm in asking Annual Meeting to talk about it."

The moderator interrupted. "I don't want us to argue about this. Let's just take a vote. All in favor of sending this query to Annual Meeting should raise their hand...now all opposed should raise their hand...it looks like the motion is defeated. Does anyone else have anything to say?"

The next year Julia submitted her query again, and again it failed. People began to talk about her, to say maybe she ought to leave things alone. What made her think she could change what the Brethren had always done? Why did she think she was right?

But Julia tried again, and she might have continued trying the following year, but something terrible happened. In late September her father died, and seven days later her mother passed away. Suddenly Julia had no one.

She was very sad and not sure what to do. Everything had changed in her life, it seemed—except Jesus.

***

1897, Grundy County, Iowa

Julia had a brother named Silas who lived in Iowa. Iowa was far from anyplace she knew, but it seemed to be the place to go, so soon she was heading off to Grundy County, Iowa, where she began to worship in a different Brethren church.

Julia discovered something surprising—the Brethren in the West weren't afraid of new ideas. Nor were they afraid of sending questions to Annual Meeting.

It wasn't long before she brought her query to her new church's council meeting. Julia was surprised to discover that the Grundy County church wanted to send her question to the district meeting and that the district meeting wanted to send her question off to Annual Meeting.

For a time Julia wondered if her dream might come true, that she might break bread for herself in the communion. She wanted to be closer to Jesus, and she thought this was one more way of obeying him. For ten straight years her question went to Annual Meeting, and every year it was either turned down or ignored or sent to a committee or put off for another year. But her church continued to encourage her—never give up, they told her.

It was 1910, the eleventh straight year for her question to come to Annual Meeting. She knew that many were tired of her question, and maybe of her. But she kept going to Annual Meeting.

The 1910 meeting was in Winona Lake, Indiana. The railroad went right to the tents for the meeting, and even though it was getting harder every year for Julia to walk around, she looked forward to seeing all her old friends from Ohio.

Once again her question came up, but this time things were different. One of the Brethren, D. C. Flory, said that Jesus had broken bread and passed the cup to the apostles, so maybe the minister should break the bread for both the men and the women. He said that it was better to be fair and so maybe no one, not the men or the women, should break the bread for themselves.

Suddenly there was a lot of talking. One man got up and pointed out that the women had always washed each other's feet. They hadn't needed a man to help them in that. Another man said that the disciples had passed the cup among themselves, so maybe it was okay for both men and women to break bread and drink from the cup without an elder. And then another man got up and said maybe everyone was too worried about performing communion perfectly and had forgotten why we share communion.

Julia couldn't believe what she was hearing. Finally, people were talking about the question, and they were reading Bible verses out loud to explain their reasons. That was exactly what she had always wanted them to do.

All the men were taking their turns speaking. Suddenly Julia knew she wanted to speak as well. It was very unusual for a woman to speak at Annual Meeting, but Julia remembered how she had been afraid when she was baptized and how she had stumbled, but the minister had told her that Jesus had already been where she was standing.

First, Julia told the people about the time she was baptized and how important it was to her to walk where Jesus walked. Then Julia reminded them that the Apostle Paul had told the Christians that if they were going to follow Jesus, they needed to break the bread and drink the cup.

"We sisters want to be followers of Jesus," Julia said. "We want to fulfill his command. We want to be in touch with Jesus. We want to do what the Bible says."

When she was through, Julia realized she was shaking. She hadn't expected to speak in front of all those people, but she felt that God wanted her to talk. Now that it was over, she stopped and stepped back to see what would happen.

It wasn't long before the Brethren voted. At first Julia wasn't sure she was hearing things right, but suddenly her friends were surrounding her, telling her that she had changed the way the Brethren did things. Julia felt the tears coming. All her life she wanted to follow Jesus the way the Bible told her to. Was it possible that finally she would be able to get even closer to Jesus by breaking bread with her sisters and sharing a cup with the women as well?

Julia celebrated communion again and again as she had always hoped, and so did Brethren women across the country. "Don't you know?" they would say when she walked by. "That's the woman who changed the Brethren. All by herself."

Julia Gilbert seemed like the kind of person whom no one would pay attention to, but she showed how important it is to study the Bible and try to be like Jesus. When she was older, she moved back to Ohio to help a niece care for her children. When that niece died unexpectedly the next year, Julia stayed and raised those children. Later she moved into the Brethren home for retired people where she lived the rest of her long life.

19
Who Will Protect the Children?

Evelyn Trostle

Marash, Syria, 1920

"The French Army is pulling out," the government official explained. "There will be no one to protect you when the killing starts again. You will have to leave Marash."

The official looked very pained and held out his arms as if he were helpless. But the missionaries, a small group of men and women, did not move. They had all come to help the Armenians, who had been persecuted by the Turks. The missionaries were Christians from many different religious backgrounds. One of them was Evelyn Trostle, a Brethren woman from Kansas.

"If we leave, the Turkish soldiers will slaughter the Armenian children," Evelyn Trostle said. "They've already killed their parents. Who will protect the children?"

"We can't help that," the official said. "We can't guarantee your safety. It's very dangerous here. We know it is not right for the Turks to kill the Armenians, but they've been doing it for years. There's nothing more we can do. Please don't argue with us."

The missionaries spoke among themselves for a moment. Their discussion did not take long.

"I'm sorry," Evelyn said. "We can't go. We just can't leave the Armenian children behind."

***

Why was Evelyn Trostle in Turkey? What was she doing there? It all began much earlier in time, back when a Brethren minister named D. L. Miller began to write books about countries far away.

Most Brethren liked to travel from state to state to attend Annual Meeting. And in the spring and fall, they would travel to love feasts in different churches in different weeks. But not many Brethren traveled across the ocean to distant countries.

D. L. Miller and his wife, however, loved to travel around the world. Some thought that D. L. Miller's travels were not a good idea, but most were excited when he wrote back to tell about what he saw. The articles were turned into books, and the books were very popular. He told the Brethren about people who needed help. Farmers in other countries needed help to learn how to grow crops better. Women in other countries were treated very poorly and people were needed to help them live a better and healthier life. And many children in other countries lived in terrible conditions and needed someone to build homes for them.

Most of all, D. L. Miller wrote about all the people who had not heard about Jesus yet. Some people grew excited and started to talk about going to those places to spread the gospel. They remembered that Jesus had told the apostles that they were to go everywhere around the world to baptize people. The Brethren knew that people from other churches were becoming missionaries and spreading comfort and hope and telling the people about Jesus. Why weren't Brethren doing this also?

Soon D. L. Miller was traveling to Brethren churches everywhere to tell about his travels. And he brought something with him called a Magic Lantern. For the first time he could show his photographs on a wall in a dark room. People had never seen anything like this. Suddenly all the places Brother Miller had told them about became real. He opened up a window to the world. And the Brethren wanted to go.

Soon many Brethren were organizing missionary groups. Brethren young and old began training and were soon going overseas to India and China. In these countries there were many people who weren't taken care of. In some places people were considered worthless and were treated cruelly, just because they were born into the wrong families. But the Brethren cared and Brethren missionaries came to treat them well. They took medicine with them and helped to heal the sick. They cooked food for the hungry. They visited those who were filled with sadness. They brought hope to people who thought no one cared about them. Most of all they brought the word about Jesus. They told people who Jesus was, and what he had done, and how he had died for them, and how he was raised from the dead. And when the people believed, the Brethren baptized them.

Brethren churches raised money to send missionaries overseas and to support them in their work. The missionaries sent back letters and stories and photographs, and these were printed in magazines to tell the Brethren back home how the work was going. There was great excitement.

Brethren learned new things by becoming missionaries. They learned they could work with other Christian groups. In America there were always great arguments about beliefs and traditions between people who belonged to one Christian church or another. But the missionaries learned to work together, because there was no time for disagreement when there were so many people in the world who had never heard about Jesus.

The Brethren missionaries wore the special clothes that all Brethren wore to set themselves apart. But they also found out in other countries that the new Christians could not wear the same Brethren clothes. It was difficult and sometimes impossible to find the right materials to make these clothes—and it did not seem to matter. They were still Christians, still Brethren, no matter what clothes they wore.

Then a call went out to all Christians to help the Armenians. The Turks were killing the Armenians not for anything they had done, but only because they were different. They wanted their country, called Turkey, to be free from every kind of person except Turks. They wanted to kill everyone who did not have that background.

In addition, most of the Turks were Muslims, and the Armenians were Christians. These two groups of people had lived together for centuries without any problems, but now the Turkish government told their people it was important to kill anyone who was not Muslim.

People around the world learned how more than a million Armenians had been forced from their homes, sent out on long journeys with no food so they would starve to death, or no coats so they would freeze to death. Sometimes the Turks simply went from house to house to kill the Armenians. The Turks said they had to kill the men or they would become soldiers and kill the Turks, but they also killed the women and the children.

All around the world people were horrified and asked if there was anything they could do. But many governments said it was out of their hands, that they could not interfere. They said it was too far away. They said there were too many other problems in the world.

Like many other Christians, Brethren wanted to help. They raised over a quarter of a million dollars to feed the starving people. But sending money and people to Turkey would not be as easy as sending people to India or China. World War I had ended. In order to get into Turkey to take care of the Armenians, the Brethren would have to get permission from the different armies that had stayed behind to protect the people.

In addition, Turkey was a Muslim country. The missionaries would not be allowed to talk about Jesus.

Because there was not enough time to train a lot of Brethren, only a few Brethren would be sent, and they would work with other Christians for the same cause.

Two of the Brethren who were sent were A. J. Culler and his wife. Another was Eva Mae Trostle.

When Eva Mae was a little girl, she decided she did not like her name, so she changed it on her own to Evelyn. She was born on a farm in Nickerson, Kansas, in 1889. She had two older brothers.

Evelyn's father, Charles Trostle, was known for his love of fast horses. However, when Evelyn was very young, he died in a horse and carriage accident. That left Evelyn's mother, Mary Trostle, to take care of the farm. It was a large farm and required a lot of work, but she never remarried and continued to take care of the farm herself.

When the children were grown they were sent to college. Not all the Brethren thought that college was a good idea, but Evelyn's mother moved the family to McPherson, Kansas, in order to live close to the Brethren college where Mary Trostle began to work around the college community.

Evelyn Trostle had a great time at college. She studied hard, but she also had fun. She enjoyed music recitals and performing dramatic readings. She took part in the May Day exercises, performing dances with streamers with a number of other college students. She was an officer with the Young Women's Christian Association. She also helped form a college group to sing at basketball games and to cheer at special events. But all the while, Evelyn also thought about what she would do after college.

During her last year as a student, Evelyn pondered a convention speaker's question: "After college—what?" And she wrote an essay for the student magazine, asking other students to follow their dreams and visions and to accomplish great things. Those who studied the Bible more, she said, should feel an even greater call to tell others the words of Jesus.

Evelyn wrote about the great missionary movement that was exciting people everywhere. And she asked what use is it to say great things if one does not live out the words. "Christian living is more powerful than Christian preaching. When we scan our horizon and see the wonderful tasks awaiting us, let us not forget our every day living. Even though the foundation to character was laid while in college, we must keep on building till the structure is finished and pronounced 'Well Done.' "

After Evelyn graduated from McPherson College, she went to the University of Kansas, and after that to the University of Chicago. She loved learning. She loved words. When she was through with college, Evelyn went back to teach at McPherson College. She taught Latin, English, and physical education for women. Soon she was the head of the English department at McPherson. Her students loved her. She wrote songs for them. They performed plays together.

Evelyn was very content. Then a terrible blow struck! Although a year had passed since World War I had ended, in 1919 influenza swept the world, killing people of all ages.

One of those who died from the flu was Evelyn's mother. The McPherson community was very sad. One of the things

Evelyn and her mother had done was to allow meetings to take place at their home near the college. And at Christmas time they invited students who lived far from their own families to travel with them to the farm for the holidays. The college passed a special resolution remembering Evelyn's mother and all she had done for the people there.

When her mother died Evelyn was lost. Since she could no longer help her mother, she wanted to help others. The Brethren magazines were full of stories about the sufferings of the Armenians. She read that the Turks were also rebelling against the European armies that occupied their country. So Evelyn stopped teaching for awhile and volunteered to go to Turkey to help the Armenians.

Evelyn left in June of 1919. She arrived in Marash and worked with the Brethren minister A. J. Culler. Evelyn and the other Christian workers built a hospital and brought in medicines to treat the women and men who had been harmed. There were eighty beds for the patients, but they saw over eight hundred patients a week.

They built a special children's hospital where thirty children could stay if they were badly hurt. Each day they treated between two hundred and three hundred Armenian children.

They built orphanages in several places, and soon these were filled as well. Because Evelyn knew how important school could be, they built schools for orphans, so they would have an education and a better life.

Homes were rebuilt. Jobs were created. Evelyn worked hard. Reports went back to Brethren in America about Armenian children who were given food and an education and hope. They learned how some Armenian children had been stolen and raised in Turkish families as servants and slaves, and how they were rescued and brought back to their own people.

But all along, the Turkish army tried to take back their country from the armies that had won the war. There were continuing political problems. Some governments who said they would help protect the Armenians went back on their word. The French government had promised to protect the Armenians in Marash. They were winning the war against the Turks. But suddenly the orders came for the French soldiers to leave the area. This meant the Turks could come and kill everyone.

In February 1920, the American workers met. There were people from several different religious groups. Many of them were women, who were in special danger from the Turkish troops. They were told they should leave with the French army, because there would be no one to protect them.

Some of the workers, who were very sick, had to leave. Others had to leave with the sick to care for them and make sure they escaped safely. But five women and four men all decided to stay. One of them was Evelyn Trostle. The nine posed for a photograph, not sure of what would happen. Some of those in the photograph had worried looks, but Evelyn smiled at the camera. She knew that Christian living is even more important than Christian preaching. She intended to stay with the orphans, no matter what.

The people of Marash were very frightened and attempted to flee. There had been one hundred and twenty-five patients in the hospital, but suddenly there were only thirteen, and these were the ones too sick to move. Many of the patients who left froze to death trying to escape over the mountains. Many others died as well.

The French army left and terrible times came. The Christian workers helped everyone they could, tending to the wounded and trying to hide people. Most of all, they stayed with the orphan children, who were innocent victims.

Evelyn Trostle saw massacres taking place. She saw people killed for no other reason than because they were born into one nationality rather than another. She saw people tortured in the streets. She saw Turkish soldiers do horrible things to the bodies of the dead people, laughing all the time. She was very afraid, but she would not leave the orphans.

Evelyn stayed. And the Turks did not harm the children. They had learned one important thing. They knew that only a few people had heard about what happened to the Armenians and had sent a lot of money, but they also knew that if even one American was killed, the Americans would put it in their newspapers, and soon American soldiers would come over to stop them. The Turkish soldiers were not afraid of unarmed Armenians, but they were afraid of people who had guns of their own.

Later A. J. Culler told the Brethren that "[Evelyn] preferred to remain by her post of duty, trusting God for protection, rather than to desert her orphans to the mercies of the cruel Turks. She is a noble example of the self-sacrificing labors of the relief workers."

Finally, when the massacres were over and they had saved all the people they could, the Armenian people told the American workers to leave—to go back to the United States and tell what they had seen. They knew that their best hope was for people around the world to know what had happened. They did not want to be forgotten.

"Go back to America and tell your friends about us, and thank them for what they have done for us!" they told Evelyn. But how could she get there? The journey was very dangerous. There was no way to get to a safe place without crossing many miles without any protection. There would be no police, no soldiers, to protect the workers. Even though her father had died in an accident with a fast horse, Evelyn knew she would have to rely on a fast horse of her own to get to safety. But she put herself in God's hands, and with other missionaries she set out.

In danger from bandits and soldiers and raiders, Evelyn Trostle rode a horse for a hundred and fifty miles across the desert. She knew that evil men had killed John Kline when he rode on horseback on his way back from helping people. She knew that the same thing might happen to her. But she was able to come safely to a railway station, and from there she took a train to safety.

When Evelyn Trostle returned to America, she immediately began to give lectures telling people about what was happening in Armenia. She raised over a million dollars from people of all different faiths.

While Evelyn was traveling about and telling people about Armenia, she met a minister named Harry Andrew Schuder who was also raising money for the Armenians. He was from the Congregational Church. They fell in love and were married, and Evelyn helped with his church. She loved the Brethren but she knew God was working with all the churches. Later, when they did not feel his church was doing enough to support the work for the Armenians, Evelyn and her husband became members of yet another church that was willing to help.

Evelyn Trostle never stopped caring about people. While her husband became an educator, she started a school for prisoners at San Quentin Prison in California. Soon the prisoners were able to go to elementary school, high school, and two years of college while in prison. And she never stopped telling about her time in Armenia.

Years later when Evelyn was a grandmother, she took her grandson to an Armenian restaurant in San Francisco. When the folks discovered who she was, they treated her with great respect. Although to this day the Turkish government has never admitted what they did to the Armenians, the Armenians have never forgotten those who helped them.

Even today there are places where people are not afraid to kill others because of their race, but they are afraid that if an American is hurt it will give them bad publicity. In Guatemala more than five million Mayan people were killed during a civil war not because they were fighting in the war, but because their government did not like Mayan people. Today Brethren Service workers accompany the Mayans to court so they can testify about what the government has done to them.

20
Not a Bomb— Not by Me!

Wilhelm Grahe and Harold Lefever

1717, Dusseldorf, Germany
Wilhelm Grahe hurt all over. As
a prisoner whose only crime
was being Brethren and wanting
to worship the way the Bible
told him, he not only worked
hard all day, but he was then
made to work long after dark
making buttons.

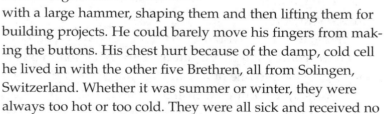

His arms and shoulders hurt
from being forced to batter rocks
with a large hammer, shaping them and then lifting them for
building projects. He could barely move his fingers from making the buttons. His chest hurt because of the damp, cold cell
he lived in with the other five Brethren, all from Solingen,
Switzerland. Whether it was summer or winter, they were
always too hot or too cold. They were all sick and received no

medical care. Indeed, those who imprisoned them expected that they would die from overwork and disease.

And now Wilhelm Grahe's legs and feet hurt as he walked toward his new prison. There were times when he thought he might fall, first to his knees and then to his face. All around him was the beauty of the European countryside: hills and valleys, tall grass, dirt paths. If he could just collapse and take a last breath, he would be received into the arms of Jesus and his suffering would be over, proving that he had been true to the Bible.

What could be better than to lie here on God's very good earth? No one would notice. Already the guards and the other prisoners were walking ahead of him. The guards trusted the Brethren who they knew were too honest to try to make the guards look bad.

But always another step.

"Please, please," said a voice near him. Wilhelm looked to his side. He could see that the man who stood next to him was a laborer. He wore well-knit but worn clothes and held out a cup of water to Wilhelm, who greedily took a drink and then coughed heavily. He took another drink.

"You are one of the prisoners?" the man asked him. "One of the Solingen Brethren?"

"Yes," Wilhelm said. "I am."

"Tell me, why don't you do what they say? Why don't you tell the court what they want to hear? Why don't you pretend to belong to one of the official churches? You could always worship God in your heart."

"Walk with me," Wilhelm said, taking a step. "I mustn't fall farther behind. Listen, brother, I sometimes think the same thing—I think to myself, Why don't I agree to go to their church so I do not have to bear this terrible burden? But I must be true to Jesus. The Bible tells us that those who are true to Jesus must sometimes suffer. And so it is."

"Lean on me," the man said. "Let me walk with you a little."

"Thank you," Wilhelm replied.

"Are those your guards?" the man asked. "I can barely see them." The man looked both ways, as if the trees and the birds might overhear their conversation. "Why don't you escape now?"

Wilhelm thought of the time Jesus told the disciples that he must do the will of God and go to Jerusalem, where he would be killed on the cross and laid in a tomb and then raised back to life. He remembered from his Bible that the Apostle Peter had told Jesus that he must not do such a thing. How that must have tempted Jesus to walk away from pain and suffering, to take the easy way. But Jesus had stayed true to God's plan.

"The guards do not worry about our running away," Wilhelm said, "because we have given our word we will not do so. We Brethren will keep our promise no matter what, and we are not afraid of what the world can do to us. We are not afraid of any person. We have not done anything wrong. We are prisoners because of the gospel of Jesus Christ. His truth and his teachings are our protection from the worst that the world can do."

Talking tired him out, and for a moment Wilhelm sank to one knee again. The man waited, and held his hand. Then the two of them set out again.

"Besides," Wilhelm said, "some day there will be others who must choose to follow the truth of Jesus Christ even if it means prison or death. If we are not true to our faith, who will they look to?"

1943, Pittsburgh, Pennsylvania

Harold R. Lefever considered himself very lucky to have a job at Westinghouse Laboratories. The rest of the world was mired in a terrible war, World War II. Many people were being drafted to fight. But Brethren were saying that the Bible did not allow them to kill other people. They felt that the Bible made it clear that all war is wrong. Harold's work on electronics at Westinghouse protected him from the draft.

Not even thirty years had passed since the last great war. At that time many Brethren were forced to decide if and how much they would cooperate with those who wanted them to fight. Some served in the military. Some served as noncombatants, meaning that they did not carry a gun, but instead worked behind the lines as medics or ambulance drivers. Still others were told by their church leaders that they could not cooperate with the Army at all. Some of those who were jailed were tortured. They were beaten, or hung up by their arms, or left to freeze or bake in prison cells. Some were not fed. Many were mistreated. Some even died.

In 1918, Brethren church leaders held a special meeting in Goshen, Indiana, to officially tell all Brethren men that they must not serve in the military. But when the government threatened to put the leaders in jail with the young men, the leaders grew afraid and took back their statement and left the younger men in jail without helping them.

After the war some of the younger men, such as Dan West and M. R. Zigler, worked with the government to make sure that the next time there was a war that Brethren, who were drafted by the Army but chose not to participate in war, could serve without having to fight and kill. People like Dan West and M. R. Zigler also went on to start programs that helped to feed people and prevent wars—programs such as CROP, Church World Service, and Heifer International.

When the Second World War started, some people believed that the war was justified and volunteered to fight. Others among Brethren, Mennonites, and Quakers believed that all war is sin and tried to serve in different ways.

Some volunteered to be guinea pigs in a starvation experiment. Through these experiments, scientists learned many things about how to bring starving people back to health. Some worked in mental hospitals and discovered horrible conditions. They determined that the people were being treated so badly that even prison would have been a better place. By taking photographs of and writing articles about the conditions, they helped to bring about change in the mental health system. Some volunteered to be smoke jumpers. They learned how to jump out of airplanes with parachutes and land to fight forest fires, thus, saving many national forests from being destroyed.

Harold was Brethren and from York, Pennsylvania. He studied electricity at Penn State and worked so hard that he graduated in three years instead of four. During that time he worked two jobs, one of them all through the night, to pay for his education. After that he went to a special school called the Massachusetts Institute of Technology, which admitted only the smartest students. He finished all his college work in a year and a half, except for one required class in German, a language he already knew.

Getting a job at Westinghouse made Harold very happy. Much of the important work on electronics was taking place there. His first job was to help invent microwave machines. (You may have a microwave oven in your home.) Harold was not only good at thinking, he was also good at doing, and the others at Westinghouse found out they could talk with Harold about ideas for a microwave antenna and he would not only improve the ideas, but he could also build the machines. He was very successful.

Then one day Harold was told he would be working on a special project. It was a secret project, so he wasn't to tell anyone about it. He would be working on one small part of a bigger project. He was told not to ask questions about the rest of the machine that was being built. He was to make this one special thing.

Even though Harold was not told what he was working on, he soon figured it out. He was working on a trigger for a bomb—not just any bomb, but an atomic bomb.

People were not really sure how powerful the bomb would be, but they knew it might be the most powerful bomb ever made. Both sides in the war were dropping many bombs. Even though it was very hard to believe at the time, some thought that one atomic bomb might be able to destroy a whole city by itself, killing hundreds of thousands of people. If enough atomic bombs were dropped, they might destroy all the life on earth. This sounded like a terrible thing.

There were some who thought that even though the bomb would be terrible, it would end the war and, though it would kill many people, it might also save many people. There were others who thought that even though they wanted to win the war, having the bomb would be too terrible a price to pay. Even today people do not agree about the atomic bomb.

At first Harold didn't say anything. He wanted to think. Working on electronics at Westinghouse kept him out of the war. But working on the trigger made him a part of the war. At that time Harold was about to be married to a woman with whom he shared a deep commitment to peace and justice. Life was good.

What mattered to Harold was that he was helping to make the bomb. He knew that whether or not he worked on the trigger, there would still be an atomic bomb. But after talking to his fiancee, Lillian, and others, he made a decision. He would resign from his job. He knew that once he resigned from his job he would be drafted, and once he was drafted, he could say he was Brethren and did not believe in participating in war. Then he could choose to work on some of the important projects that other Brethren were working on—in mental hospitals, on farms, or in medical programs. He could choose to fight fires on the ground or in the air. Or he could help grow food for hungry people around the world.

But Harold believed that if he did any of these things he would still be helping the war effort. So he resigned from his job and wrote to his draft board telling them that he was now eligible for the draft but that he would not serve. He also gave them his address so they could find him.

Then he and Lillian got married. They were married on a Saturday, and on Monday the marshals came and took him to the federal courthouse in Scranton, Pennsylvania. Although he was soon let out to wait for his trial, he knew that it would not be long before he was sentenced to prison.

Throughout his trial Harold was very polite and helpful to his guards, to the lawyers, and to the judge, because he believed, as the Bible says, that Christians must observe the rules of the government whenever it is possible, even if that government does not agree with what Jesus teaches. But that also meant that, if necessary, one must disobey the government and take the punishment to show how to live like Jesus.

On October 25, 1943, Harold Lefever stood before the judge and explained why he would not help with the war. Harold wrote it all down on a piece of paper and then read it aloud.

"War is a great evil," Harold told the judge. He said that even when people are trying to fix a terrible problem, war only makes things worse.

"There really are no enemies at all," he said, trusting in the method of loving one's enemies. And then he told the judge that as long as Americans are mistreating black people and Jews and others, and the rich people are taking advantage of the poor, then it was wrong to try to fix other countries.

"There is a better way than war," he also said. Harold reminded the judge how Jesus told people to turn the other cheek and to love their enemies. The way of suffering love for enemies has been demonstrated to be the only effective way to reconciliation. This was the way used by Jesus Christ in his day and to which his life is the greatest testimony.

Now the judge had to decide what to do with this man who seemed to be very smart and was polite, but who would not do what the Army wanted him to do. The judge decided that since it was normal to serve two years in the Army, Harold Lefever would have to serve two years in prison.

Harold thought about what happened to those who went to prison in the First World War. He did not know what would happen to him in prison, but he knew it could be a very dangerous place. Only the worst criminals are supposed to go to prison. But he had said that he would rather live like Jesus than do what the government told him to do, so he was sent to the federal prison in Ashland, Kentucky.

It wasn't long before those in charge of the prison learned that Harold Lefever was very good with electricity and knew how to make things. Soon he was made a trustee and allowed to come and go through the prison gates to do work on the electrical system. Like Wilhelm Grahe many centuries before, Harold Lefever could have escaped any time he wanted to. However, he wanted to show that people who follow Jesus are not afraid of the punishment that comes from the world—that they serve Jesus only.

Less than a year later Harold Lefever was released from prison. He was sent to a hospital near Washington, D.C., to serve the rest of

his sentence doing work there. Lillian was allowed to come live with him.

After the war Harold Lefever continued to work for peace and justice. He went to Washington D.C., for the civil rights march led by Dr. Martin Luther King, Jr. He spoke out against war. He helped his community organize better ways of disposing of garbage and taking better care of the earth. He tried to serve Jesus all the days of his life.

Wilhelm Grahe and the rest of the Solingen Brethren were released from prison in 1720, thanks to the prayers and efforts of many Brethren and Mennonites. Grahe and the rest of the prisoners were so weak that they had to be taken back home by cart.

21
A Secret Weapon

Helena Kruger

Austria, 1946

The war was over in Europe. But
there was no peace. Although
the German armies had surrendered and no one was dropping
bombs anymore, people were
living among the ruins everywhere. There wasn't enough
food, and many people were
very sick.

Terrible things had been done
during the war. The leadership
of the German government had murdered millions of
people, trying to wipe out the Jewish population of Europe.
Some of the German people knew nothing of all this, but
many others had helped this happen.

Many people had lost loved ones and their homes, so
there was a great bitterness against the German people.
Though many adults had done terrible things, certainly the

children had done nothing wrong. Still, children had suffered greatly during the war, and now German children were still suffering.

It was one thing to win a war. It was even harder to win a peace. After the First World War, the losers were treated so badly that the Second World War broke out nearly thirty years later. This time there were people who hoped to change things after the war. Was it possible for the Germans and the Americans to become friends? If they could become friends, they might never fight a war against each other again.

Many Brethren tried to help. Dan West started Heifer International when he sent live milk cows to the hungry people of Europe. There were Brethren peacemakers like Ralph Smeltzer and M. R. Zigler, who had already done much work for peace. For instance, Ralph Smeltzer left his job as a teacher to try to help the Japanese Americans who were unfairly rounded up and put into camps. When America and Japan went to war against each other, some people insisted that all Americans of Japanese descent were dangerous and had to be put away. Many Japanese Americans lost their homes and their possessions. Ralph Smeltzer, his wife, Mary Blocher Smeltzer, and others helped set up schools for the children in these camps and later helped to resettle families in new homes and new jobs.

M. R. Zigler helped make it possible for Brethren and other Christians who did not believe in fighting wars to serve people in peaceful ways. He helped to arrange for these people to work on farms, to take part in medical experiments, or to put out fires, instead of going into the Army.

Their efforts were especially difficult because others did not want to help the Germans or people of German descent. It didn't matter if they had fought in the war or not. People hated them simply because they were German. In Austria, for instance, people who were descended from Germans were not allowed to go to the hospital. They were not given housing. They were not given food. Fortunately, Zigler and Smeltzer had a "secret weapon" for peace.

That secret weapon was Helena Kruger. Helena had been born in Siberia. When she was a teenager, her family fled from Russia after the Communists took over. She knew what it was like to lose a home and possessions. She knew what it was like to be a refugee.

Helena also knew what it was like to receive help. She and her family had first moved to Germany, but soon they were given help to come to America. She and her husband settled in Annville, Pennsylvania, where they ran a dairy farm. They were members of the Spring Creek Church of the Brethren.

Everyone knew that Helena Kruger was very good at getting things done. She could also speak English, German, Russian, Polish, and Dutch. So the Brethren decided to send Helena Kruger to Austria in 1946 to win the peace and help the people.

There was just one problem. It took all four of them, Helena, her husband, Peter, and their two sons, to run the dairy farm. The cows on a dairy farm must be milked twice a day, every day. Because the cows do not take a day off, the farmers cannot take a day off. If Helena Kruger were to leave to help the Brethren in Austria, then her husband and her two sons would have even more work to do. So Helena said she could not go.

But her husband, Peter, was thankful that churches had taken care of them. He knew now that it was time for the family to take care of others. He said that if the church had not helped them come to America, the Kruger family would still be homeless. He also said that when the church calls people to serve, then they need to go if it is God's will.

So Helena Kruger went to Austria where she tried to help the people of German ancestry. These were the people who were very sick and very hungry. It didn't matter if they had fought in the war or not. People hated them because they were German. They blamed them for the war.

In Austria Helena saw signs of the terrible war everywhere. Buildings lay in ruins. People were wandering around with nowhere to go. Tuberculosis, a terrible disease of the lungs, was spreading everywhere, especially among the children. Many had no hope.

Helena Kruger helped to supervise the task of providing food and shelter. She was not afraid to ask for what she needed. She would not leave the officials alone. Whenever she saw extra materials and supplies lying around, she would ask for them. Sometimes she would not wait for an answer, but took them anyway and started using them.

There were many armies in Austria and all over Europe. Some of the soldiers were American, some Russian, some British, and some were French. They all soon learned that Helena Kruger did not know the meaning of the word no.

Because she could speak many languages, she could talk with nearly everyone. Soon everyone knew her and knew that she came to work in the name of Jesus. Everyone trusted her. When she would ride up in her car to a gate or checkpoint, the people would say, "Here comes the church!" and let her pass through.

She went wherever she wanted in order to get the things she needed, and she accomplished much. One American officer said he could have been put on trial for giving supplies to Helena Kruger, but that it wasn't possible to tell her no!

Helena Kruger knew that children come first and that children need hope. She knew the German children needed a school there in Austria. If they did not go to school, they would not have any hope. They would grow up full of hatred that could lead to another war as terrible as the one just ended. So she started by building a kindergarten.

First she found an old building that was blackened from smoke damage. She found windows that were soon put into place to keep out the wind. She got the building cleaned up. If she needed help, Helena Kruger asked some of the German parents, because she knew they wanted a school for their children. She found extra wood in warehouses to use for making repairs. She found equipment. She found teachers. Soon the school was underway.

Because German children were not allowed to go to the Austrian hospitals, Helena once again found a place to set up a hospital and began to ask for supplies. She found beds and tables and mattresses and blankets and sheets and pillowcases. She found clothes for the nurses. She found extra food. And she found gasoline, which was very scarce, so the hospital could have an ambulance. She found paint and thermometers and wash basins. Soon the hospital was open.

The German people in Austria also had no homes. The Austrian people didn't want to share their homes with the Germans. And no one wanted to sell property to the Germans, even if they had money—but most of them didn't. One day Helena was driving by an old railroad yard. The bombs had hit in that area, and there were many burned and wrecked railroad cars. But some still had walls and a roof.

Helena Kruger had an idea. Why not turn these railroad cars into houses? People could live in them. But they were so large, she couldn't just take them. She would have to get permission. First, she asked someone from the American Army, who said she had to talk to the local mayor, who said she needed to talk to the man who ran the railroad yards. And guess what! He said she had to talk to the American Army.

By now Helena Kruger could tell that none of these people wanted to make a decision. They didn't care. They just wanted her to go away. But, instead, Helena brought together the mayor and the man who ran the railroad yards and the man who ran the American Army. She made them talk about turning the railroad cars into houses, and she did not leave until they gave her permission.

Soon twenty-six railroad cars were turned into homes. The German people worked hard on these homes. They worked so hard that the Austrian people hired them to work for the railroad company. Before that, they had been saying that the Germans were no good. Now they wanted to work with them!

Helena Kruger was also waiting for the American government to send food to help her in her work. She was waiting for the Brethren to send food. Nothing was coming. So she wrote to her own church, the Spring Creek Church of the

Brethren in Pennsylvania, and asked them to send 1,440 eggs that were about to hatch and 65 sacks of feed for the chickens. Her church took up a collection and soon the chickens were on their way. Before long, those chickens grew up and were laying eggs for the hungry people.

Helena Kruger's story would not be complete without this one. Helena Kruger was afraid of no one—not even the Russians. And everyone was afraid of the Russians!

On this particular occasion, the car spluttered and whined to a stop as the burly Russian guards waved it to a halt at the checkpoint. For a moment the two men stared at the car and then lowered their rifles to point them at the driver. They were very suspicious. Millions of Russian people had died in the war against the Germans. Now the Russians did not trust the Germans. They did not even trust the Americans, even though they had fought together against the Germans. The Russians did not trust anybody.

After the war the armies that had won the war each occupied parts of countries that had been held captive by the Germans, such as Austria, and watched over them. The people living in the Russian zone of Austria were treated badly and were afraid they would not have freedom there, so many of them tried to escape from the Russian side of the country to the American side. As cars came and went, the Russians were always watching for people who might be trying to escape.

The guards thought for a moment that they might ask the driver to get out of the car. They considered opening the trunk to see if there was anything valuable inside, because they would take valuable things when they could.

Then one of the guards relaxed and smiled and tapped the other.

"It's all right," he said, in Russian. "She's okay. It's Mrs. Kruger."

The wind blew cold past their threadbare coats. The one guard looked puzzled.

"Why do you say she's okay? She's an American, right?" He knew that the Russians guards were not supposed to trust the Americans.

"She's not like most Americans. She can speak Russian. And she is nice to us."

The guard waved at the car so the driver would know to keep going. But Helena Kruger got out of the car and began to talk to the guards in Russian.

She asked them how they felt. She asked them about their families, about their wives and children. She made jokes with them in Russian. When they told her about their children, she went back to the car and pulled out some chocolate bars. She asked them to send the candy to their children for her.

The Russian guards were very glad to get the candy. Now that the war was over, there was not enough food to go around, and certainly there was no candy. They knew their children would be very happy.

"Thank you! Thank you!" they said in Russian as she finally drove away. The Russian guards never checked her car. They did not look in the trunk. They did not know that Helena Kruger was smuggling people out of the Russian zone and into the American zone. They were squeezed inside her car, afraid to make a sound, afraid they might be sent to a Russian prison and never be seen again.

Everywhere Helena went, people were glad to see her. She helped the children. She helped their families. She didn't care about a person's background. She knew God loves everybody the same.

For the rest of her life Helena Kruger helped the Brethren. After her work was finished in Austria, she worked in Greece and later at the Brethren Service Center in New Windsor, Maryland. There she worked to help refugees (people without homes) from around the world get settled in America. Because she spoke many languages, she often worked as a translator.

Because of Helena Kruger and many people like her, the Germans and the Americans are no longer enemies. They no longer go to war against each other.

Helena Kruger's husband, Peter, died in 1956. She was very sad, but she continued to work to help the Brethren. She moved to the Brethren Service Center in New Windsor, Maryland, and continued her work there. She died in 1978.

22
The Man Who Could Change Lives

M. R. Zigler

1981, Camp Anywhere
"Time for s'mores!" said the
camp leader. The campfire was
burning brightly as the skies got
darker. Galen and Connie
Brubaker, brother and sister,
were sitting together, shivering
just a little. It was the middle of
summer, but at camp it sometimes got chilly after the sun
went down.

Trees circled the campfire
ring. The light from the fire danced on every rill and whorl
of their bark, making it look as if the trees themselves were
shivering with the campers. There were only a few stars
bright enough to shine around the leaves that stretched up to
the sky.

There was smoke everywhere, but Galen knew that smoke drove away the mosquitoes that came out at night. Not that they bothered him. Mom always sent along plenty of mosquito repellant.

Mosquitoes were about the only thing bad about camp. Everything else was great. They'd been waiting months for this week to come, and now that it was here, they weren't about to let little things spoil it for them.

Only a few moments ago they were singing their favorite camp songs, the ones they'd sung a year ago, their first year at camp. They had continued to sing some of them around home afterwards until everyone, even they themselves, had grown sick of them.

I'm a little striped skunk,
Sleeping under someone's bunk
Nobody wants to sleep with me
'cause I'm as smelly as can be!
> *Second verse, same as the first,*
> *A little bit louder and a little bit worse!*

That song had grown louder and louder with each repetition, until the campers were all so hoarse they finally had to stop. And there were other favorites that followed, fun songs like the one about the "grand old Duke of York," where you had to jump up and down. And there were church songs like "Wade in the Water" that you never sang at church.

Connie was glad to see that some of the kids who had been scared the day before when they arrived at camp, first-timers who had never been away from home before, had forgotten their tears and were smiling and hollering with every-one else.

She watched as the new kids took the marshmallows and sticks from the camp leader and timidly approached the fire to melt them. There was Alyssa Stutsman, who was from her church. She had tried to go back home with her mom and dad when they finished registering her for camp yesterday afternoon. Tonight she was holding the stick out as far as she could, as if she wasn't sure if the fire would jump out and get her.

Galen was helping another one of the new kids, Kenny Carroll, with his marshmallows, holding out the graham crackers stacked with chocolate bars and smashing them over the hot, soft marshmallows and pulling them off the stick.

"Go ahead," Galen was saying. "S'mores are good. Hold on tight. It's not too hot."

"Why do they call them s'mores?" Kenny asked.

Connie leaned over and said, "Because after you eat one, you want some more. Get it? S'mores?"

Connie and Galen could see Bill, the camp leader, talking to an older grownup, a man with white hair and a black coat. They didn't know who he was, but they'd seen him come into camp earlier in the day. The leaders treated him like he was someone special, but he sat down with the kids and ate lunch of wieners, beans, and a cup of fruit. Then he had gone off with the camp counselors during rest time and spent awhile talking to them.

The man was friendly with everyone. Now he was hold-ing his own stick and roasting some marshmallows. One of them caught fire, and he laughed. When he made his s'more, he handed it to one of the children who had dropped her stick into the fire by accident.

The camp leader raised his hand for everyone to get quiet. Connie raised her hand and glared at Galen, so he raised his hand and stopped talking, too. One by one the other kids saw what was happening and quieted down.

"I want to make an announcement," the camp leader said. He took another look at their visitor, and Galen wasn't sure what his look meant. "We have a special guest with us. Perhaps you saw him around earlier today. His name is M. R. Zigler—your parents and your grandparents all know his name. He was talking to your counselors earlier today about something called BVS, but Brother Zigler said he would like to talk to you as well. I told him it's been a long day and he should talk for about ten minutes before it's time for us to get back to our cabins. Let's give him our attention."

Brother Zigler smiled the moment he stepped up. Galen wondered what he would say.

"Your leader thought that I should not be talking to you, that you are too young. But I came here to talk to your counselors about BVS—Brethren Volunteer Service—and what a difference they could make in the world, and how they could help make this a peaceful world. But I also wanted to talk to you, because I know you are never too young to make a difference—to bring peace."

Galen wasn't too sure what to make of this man's speech. He could see the camp leader was very uncomfortable about Brother Zigler. Most of all, he wondered how he could make a difference. He was only eleven years old, and there didn't seem to be much he could do by himself.

"Don't let anyone tell you you're too young," M. R. Zigler was saying, as if he had read Galen's mind. "Now I'm going to show you how you can make a difference for peace in the world—and how you can start today. How many of you have ever heard of Heifer Project International?"

Right away Connie dug her elbow into Galen's side, and even though it was getting dark, he could tell she was smiling. She liked knowing the right answer. Quickly she raised her hand and spoke before anyone called on her.

"I've heard of it," Connie said. "We raised money for Heifer Project in our Sunday school. They even brought a lot of animals to the church so we could see how we were helping people in faraway places."

"Very good," Mr. Zigler said, standing by the campfire. As the flames flickered, a pattern of dark shadows mixed with light danced over all of them, including their speaker.

"Well, one of the causes of war is hunger. If we feed people, they are able to take care of themselves. Heifer Project sends live animals that will give birth to more animals to people who are hungry. Instead of giving people a meal that they eat only once and then it's gone, they send them a cow who gives milk or a goat whose milk goes for cheese or a chicken that lays eggs. Suddenly they can take care of themselves and their family, and they feel good about themselves. Then the next time one of their leaders tries to tell them to go to war they're not interested."

Brother Zigler paused for just a moment. "Think about it. We fought two big wars against Germany in this century, but that won't happen again. The German people got heifers like everyone else. They're good people—they're happy people.

And they're not hungry people. Every one of you who raises money for Heifer Project at your church or in your family is helping prevent wars.

"The man who started Heifer Project was a Brethren fellow named Dan West. Dan was a young man who was helping hungry people in Spain during the Second World War. There wasn't enough milk to go around, and he knew children were going to die and that the families who were hungry would go on fighting the war. He kept thinking there had to be a way to get some of those cows from his home state of Indiana all the way across the ocean to Europe.

"Fortunately, Dan West was young and full of ideas. Someone else might have told him his ideas were crazy, but I told him to go ahead, we'd find a way to fund them. And after the big war was over, Dan West got a lot of other people excited about sending live animals, and after they got over thinking he was crazy, they all realized he was just about the smartest man there was. You know, Dan West was ahead of his time. He was always ahead of everyone, and because of him we did a lot of things even before we got permission to do them. But once we got started with something like Heifer Project, it couldn't be stopped. And later, after others were done criticizing us, they all said it was a great idea."

Bill, the camp leader, got up, cleared his throat, and announced, "It's getting to be about time for the kids to go to their cabins."

"How many of you want to go to bed?" Mr. Zigler asked. No one raised their hands. "Then I'll only talk a minute or two more," he said. The camp leader rolled his eyes, but he sat down.

"I remember when I was a boy that we had a guest room, and I learned from my mother that there was always room to help someone. Whether they were people famous among the Brethren or just folks who were down on their luck and looking for work, my mother made sure they got a good meal at our table and had a warm bed to sleep in. Everyone was welcome. That's because every person is one of God's children.

"Later, during the First World War, I went to Parris Island to help take care of the soldiers, because I wasn't going to be a soldier and kill people. I watched them train those boys to use their bayonets to stab people, to kill them, and I wondered, why can't we put the same effort into training people for peace just like we train them for war? That's why I always try to talk to you young people wherever I go. I want you to work as hard for peace as some people work for war."

"Young people have always made a difference," Mr. Zigler continued, "and it seems like older folks try to figure out ways to stop them. All of you should think big and plan big, like a Dan West. We want to feed the hungry. We want to stop wars. That's what the Brethren Service Committee was all about. That's what On Earth Peace is all about. Countries spend millions of dollars training people to kill each other, and we want to spend just thousands of dollars to train people for peace. Every one of you can be trained for peace. You don't have to go to war. That's why we have worked so hard so you can be conscientious objectors without having to go to jail."

One boy raised his hand, and said, "My mom says the reason people don't want to go to war is because they're chicken."

One of the counselors stood up, as if he was going to scold the boy, but Brother Zigler just laughed.

"Chicken? Do you think it's chicken to jump out of an airplane using an old parachute so you can drop into the middle of the woods to fight a raging fire? Is that chicken? Or how about volunteering to be a medical guinea pig, agreeing to let some scientist nearly starve you to death so they can figure out how to feed hungry people after a war without killing them? Did you know that some folks let themselves be injected with new drugs to see how they worked and if they would have bad side effects? Because that's what some Brethren young people did instead of going to war to kill people. Chicken? I think it takes courage to work for peace, especially when people look down on you and make fun of you because you want to follow Jesus instead of a government. This is why I worked so hard with the government before World War II, so our boys could show they were brave without killing anyone. Some even gave up their lives, men like Chandler Edwards and Ted Studebaker, who died in Southeast Asia during the Vietnam era."

Mr. Zigler coughed for a moment, then coughed again. "See, the old folks only know how to do things the old way. You're young. You can figure out a new way. Ask yourself, What will you be doing in twenty years? in two years? Will you be happy doing what you're doing, and will it matter? Never let anyone say you are the church of tomorrow. You are the church of today."

He had talked for a long time, much longer than anyone expected. Galen saw that the camp leader looked at his watch more than once and tried to get Mr. Zigler to look at him, but it didn't seem to matter.

Connie listened, and even though she knew some of what Mr. Zigler was talking about, it was like it was brand new, and it was about her, too. Connie often brought money to Sunday school for Heifer Project, because the Sunday school teacher said she should, but she'd never really known what it was about.

And the teacher at the regular school said that war was the only way to settle problems, but now Mr. Zigler was talking about ways to change people's lives so there would never be a war in the first place.

"Listen, just one last thing," he said at last. "I've worked with a lot of churches, a lot of other Christian churches, and I've told them that if we want to stop war, then all we have to do as Christians is to stop killing each other. That would stop half the wars right there. That's what I say: Let the Christians of the world promise not to kill each other. Now I want all of you to think about working for peace. Thank you, and I'll see you in the morning."

The camp leader stood up extra fast and led them in singing "Taps."

Day is done,
Gone the sun,
From the from the lake, from the hills, from the sky.
All is well, safely rest.
God is nigh.

"See you in the morning," Connie said as she waved goodnight to Galen. "I'm going to raise a lot of money for Heifer Project," she added, "more than anyone ever has at the church."

"Not if I raise more money," Galen replied. He stopped and watched Mr. Zigler walking very slowly with his cane toward the cabin. Mr. Zigler stopped one of the counselors and started to talk to him. Galen realized it was Jimmy Bittinger, his cabin counselor.

It didn't take long for Galen to get ready for bed. Soon he was inside his sleeping bag, listening to the other boys talking, none of them really sleepy yet. When Jimmy Bittinger returned, everyone waved their flashlights at him, causing him to raise his hands over his face.

"You all ready for bed?" he asked the boys.

"Hey, what did Mr. Zigler talk to you about?" someone asked.

Jimmy shrugged. "Well, I thought I was going to go from college to law school. But now I think I'm going to join Brethren Volunteer Service for a couple of years before I continue with my education."

"That man *made* you do that?" someone asked in amazement.

"No, I want to. I want to do that now. The more he talked about it, the more I realized how important it is to live your faith, to do what Jesus says and not what people say. I really want to go!" Jimmy said almost as if he couldn't believe it.

"Who was that man, anyway?" asked another boy.

"That's the man who can get you to do anything," Jimmy said. "He's the most important man in the Brethren. Just about everything we've done that's been any good, he's been a part of it. In all the ways we help people for Jesus, all the ways we stand up for peace, Mr. Zigler has had something to do with it."

The next day at breakfast M. R. Zigler sat down across the table from Galen.

"I could see you were really paying attention last night," Mr. Zigler said. "What's your name?"

"Galen Brubaker," he replied.

"Well, Galen, I just want to remind you that you can make a big difference. We've got to get everyone to work together, and we need you and everyone like you to help make peace in the world. There are millions training for war, and only a few people training for peace. But this is what God wants us to do. What do you say?"

Galen was surprised that Mr. Zigler not only seemed to know him, but he trusted him and wanted him to do important things. And he began to realize he wanted to do those important things. Suddenly it seemed possible to work for peace.

"I say yes, Mr. Zigler," Galen answered. "I say, yes, I'm going to work for peace."

Michael Robert (M. R.) Zigler was born in Virginia in a house near the home owned by John Kline. He loved Brethren history and he believed in making peace. Some people called him "Mr. Brethren." He was one of the most important Brethren to ever live.

He worked in almost every major Brethren program of the twentieth century to help people in the name of Jesus. M. R. Zigler was the head of the programs that built hospitals and schools and fed people in Europe, helping people get back on their feet after the Second World War. He worked with other churches and the government so Brethren could work for peace instead of going to war. He insisted that Brethren work with other churches for peace, and he was respected and admired by church leaders around the world. He arranged a handshake between the leaders of the Brethren groups that had split apart, and this led to the publication of The Brethren Encyclopedia. *He trusted the young people to do the work of the church around the world.*

No one knows just how much he did for the church and for peace.

Acknowledgments

There are those who think that books for children are different from other books and that one has to write in a special language, with a special tone, but I have always believed that a good children's book is a good book. I have tried to write the sort of book I would like to read.

Thank you, first of all, to my parents, Frank and Dee Ramirez, for reading stories to me when I was very young. Thank you also to my older sister, Mary Ann Hodge, who told us stories about "The Seven Bad Pigs." They have always provided a model of how a good story is made.

I want to thank the authors of Brethren histories, people such as Roger Sappington, Martin Grove Brumbaugh, Henry Holsinger, Carl Bowman, and especially Donald F. Durnbaugh for his source books and for *Fruit of the Vine*, the best history of the Church of the Brethren.

I want to thank Susan Taylor, librarian of McPherson College; Marlin Heckman, librarian of the University of La Verne; archival intern Denise Kettering; Marlene Neher; Paul Roth; Faye Ellen Winger; and Connie Enzminger for helping me find information for this book.

Thank you to Julie Garber, Nancy Klemm, Wendy McFadden, and Russ Matteson of Brethren Press for their confidence in this idea. And a special thanks to Keith Morse who read some of these stories and told me he liked them.

A special thank you to Tim Harvey who, when I described this book to him, told me all about Cain Lackey, who in turn provided the title story of this collection! Thanks also to Wil

Nolan, a descendant of Lackey, for providing some very colorful additions to that history.

Most of all, I want to thank Ken Shaffer, archivist of the Brethren Historical Library and Archives, for tracking down innumerable documents, and historian Don Durnbaugh for answering my many questions about Brethren history.

Frank Ramirez
Everett, Pennsylvania

Illustration Credits

The illustrations and photographs at the beginning of each chapter have been adapted for this book by Gwen Stamm of Scottdale, Pennsylvania.

1. Painting by Guy Wolek, from the cover of *Heritage and Promise: Perspectives on the Church of the Brethren* by Emmert F. Bittinger. Copyright © 1983 Brethren Press, Elgin, Illinois.
2. From panel 1 of the Medford D. Neher mural at Camp Alexander Mack, Milford, Indiana.
3. G. L. Croome drawing from Peter Nead's Theological Writings of 1850. Courtesy of Brethren Historical Library and Archives (BHLA).
4. Photo of the Brother House at Ephrata Cloister, Ephrata, Pennsylvania. Courtesy of BHLA.
5. Painting No. 19 by Albert Winkler for "Come Up Higher," 250th Anniversary filmstrip. Copyright © 1958 the General Brotherhood Board, Church of the Brethren. Courtesy of BHLA.
6. Painting No. 18 by Albert Winkler for "Come Up Higher," 250th Anniversary filmstrip. Copyright © 1958 the General Brotherhood Board, Church of the Brethren. Courtesy of BHLA.
7. Illustration of Henry Kurtz by Kermon Thomasson. Courtesy of BHLA.
8. Painting No. 31 by Albert Winkler for "Come Up Higher," 250th Anniversary filmstrip. Copyright ©

1958 the General Brotherhood Board, Church of the Brethren. Courtesy of BHLA.

9. Photo of Dr. P. R. Wrightsman from *Brethren Family Almanac*, 1915. Courtesy of BHLA.

10. Photo of Ann Rowland from *Sidelights of Brethren History* by Freeman Ankrum. Copyright © 1962 Brethren Press, Elgin, Illinois.

11. Photo of John H. Bowman. Courtesy of BHLA.

12. G. L. Croome drawing of curious onlookers observing the Brethren love feast. From Peter Nead's Theological Writings of 1850. Courtesy of BHLA.

13. Photo of John Lewis. Courtesy of BHLA.

14. Photo of David Emmert from *The Brethren Encyclopedia*, Vol. 1. Courtesy of BHLA.

15. Photo of the John Kline home in Linville Creek, Virginia. Courtesy of BHLA.

16. Photo of Abraham Harley Cassel. Courtesy of BHLA.

17. Photo of Cain Lackey at the age of 30 from *The Biography of Cain Lackey* by Joel B. Naff, © 1976. Courtesy of BHLA.

18. Photo of Julia Gilbert. Courtesy of BHLA.

19. Photo of Evelyn Trostle in Marash, Syria, in 1920. From *The Lions of Marash* by Stanley E. Kerr. Copyright © 1973.

20. Photo of Harold Lefever from *Messenger,* January 1975. Copyright © 1975 Church of the Brethren General Board.

21. Photo of Helena Kruger by J. Henry Long. Courtesy of BHLA.

22. Photo of M. R. Zigler. Courtesy of BHLA.